success

at Key Stage 3
English

Steve Eddy and Mary Hartley

with Tony Buzan

Hodder & Stoughton

A MEMBER OF THE HODDER HEADLINE GROUP

Acknowledgements

The publishers would like to thank the following for permission to reproduce material in this volume:

Victor Gollancz: *Z for Zachariah* by Robert O'Brien, and *The Friends* by Rosa Guy; Scholastic Ltd: *Northern Lights* Text © Philip Pullman, 1995, first published by Scholastic Ltd; HarperCollins Publishers: *Raven's Knot* by Robin Jarvis; Oxford University Press: *Brother in the Land* by Robert Swindells; *Beowulf* translated by David Wright, reprinted by permission of the Peter Fraser & Dunlop Group Ltd; Macmillan Children's Books Ltd; *The Car* by Gary Paulsen; Hamish Hamilton: *Flour Babies*, © Anne Fine, 1992, reproduced by Penguin Books Ltd; *The Village by the Sea* Copyright © Anita Desai, 1982. Reproduced by permission of the author c/o Rogers, Coleridge & White Ltd, 20 Powis Mews, London W11 1JN; Random House: *Cider with Rosie* by Laurie Lee; Virago Press: *Her People* by Kathleen Dayus, and 'Woman Work' from *And I Still Rise* by Maya Angelou; Enid Blyton Limited: *The Story of My Life* by Enid Blyton; Andre Deutsch Ltd; *The Blyton Phenomenon* by Sheila Ray; Reed Books: *A Childhood at Green Hedges* by Imogen Smallwood; Windrush Press Ltd: *The Secret Diary of Sarah Thomas* edited by June Lewis; Bradt Publications: *Guide to Cuba* by Stephen Fallon: BBC Worldwide: extract reproduced from *Our Man in ...* by Clive Anderson reproduced with permission, © Clive Anderson 1995; QUIT: Break Free; Guardian: 'Love the Piggy Within', 'Tamworth One Cops it in Copse', *Guardian*, 17 January 1998; Heinemann Educational Publishers: 'Little Rosebud Girl' by Anson Gonzalez, and 'A Song for England' by Andrew Salkey, from *Caribbean Poetry*; Faber and Faber: 'The Warm and the Cold' from *The Seasons Songs* by Ted Hughes, and 'Twelve Songs XI Roman Wall Blues' from *Collected Poems* by W H Auden.

The publishers would also like to acknowledge the following for use of their material:

Amryl Johnson: 'Granny in de Market Place', by Amryl Johnson, from the *Heinemann Book of Caribbean Poetry*; David Higham Associates: *Stung from a Sense of Shame* by Jan Needle; Penguin Books Ltd: *Walkabout* by James Vance Marshall; Puffin Books Ltd: *The Endless Steppe* by Esther Hautzig; Anchor Press/Doubleday: 'Frankie Mae' by Jean Wheeler Smith, from *Black-eyed Susans*; Viking Books: *Zlata's Diary* by Zlata Filipovic; New Holland Books: *Globetrotter Travel Guide, Cuba*; Livewire/The Woman's Press: *French Leave* by Eileen Fairweather; National Back Pain Association; Bristol Hippodrome; RSPCA; Oxford University Press: 'Skivers' by David Williams, from *Sport* edited by John Foster; Random Century Group: 'The Bicycle Ride' by Selima Hill, from *Six Women Poets*.

Every effort has been made to trace and acknowledge ownership of copyright. The publishers will be glad to make suitable arrangements with any copyright holders whom it has not been possible to contact.

Photo acknowledgements
R.D. Battersby/Bosun: p.87

ISBN 0 340 72509 5

First published 1998

| Impression number | 10 9 8 7 6 5 4 3 2 1 |
| Year | 2001 2000 1999 1998 |

Designed and produced by Gecko Ltd, Bicester, Oxon
Printed in Great Britain for Hodder & Stoughton Educational, a division of Hodder Headline Plc, 338 Euston Road, London NW1 3BH by Scotprint Ltd, Musselburgh, Scotland.

Mind Maps: Peter Bull and Chris Rothero
Illustrations: Peter Bull, Harvey Collins, Dave Mostyn, Micheal Ogden, John Plumb, Chris Rothero and Nick Ward
Cover design: Amanda Hawkes
Cover illustration: Paul Bateman

Contents

Shortcuts to success

Would you like your homework to be fun and a lot easier? Would you like to be able to remember things better? Would you like to read faster and understand more? To find out how, read the next three pages and follow the suggestions throughout this book.

Your *amazing* brain

Your brain is like a super, *super*, SUPER computer. The world's best computers have only a few thousand chips. Your brain has brain cells – 12 *million* MILLION of them! This means you are a genius just waiting to discover yourself! All you have to do is learn how to get those brain cells working together, and you'll not only do better at school, you'll do your homework more quickly and therefore have more free time too.

Your *magnificent* 'Memory Muscle'

Your memory is like a muscle. If you don't use it, it will grow weaker and weaker, but if you do keep it exercised, it will grow stronger and stronger.

Here are four tips for improving your Memory Muscle:

1 Work for between 20 and 40 minutes at a time, and *then take a break*

The break allows your Memory Muscle to rest and lets the information sink in. This also makes your Memory Muscle stronger for your next learning session.

2 Go back over your work

If you wait for a little while after you have been learning something, and you then look back at it later, you'll catch your brain at the top of the memory wave and remember even more.

3 Make connections

Your Memory Muscle becomes stronger when it can link things together. You can use your brain's amazing power to conjure up a huge number of pictures and ideas at once to help you to remember information. Join the separate facts together in some way to make a picture, for example on a Mind Map, and they'll come back to you all together, in a flash!

4 Think BIG

Your Memory Muscle gets stronger if what it is trying to remember is special in some way, so 'think big' and make what you are learning brightly coloured, funny, peculiar, special.

Your new *magic* learning formula – The Mind Map

When people go on holidays or journeys they take maps to give them a general picture of where they are going and to help them find their way around when they get there. It is exactly the same with your memory and schoolwork. If you have a 'map' of what you have to cover, everything is easier.

The Mind Map is a very special map. It helps you to find your way around a subject easily and quickly because it mirrors the way your brain works. Use it for organising your work both at school and at home, for taking notes and planning your homework.

The Mind Maps in this book

Below you will see a Mind Map on the media.

In the centre of this Mind Map is a picture of a television, which summarises the theme of the topic. Coming out from this there are six branches, each one covering an important part of the topic.

You see how easy it is! You have summarised an entire topic on just one page, and this is now firmly logged in your brain, for you to get at whenever you want! If you look at this Mind Map five times over the next five months, the information it contains will be in your brain for many, many years to come.

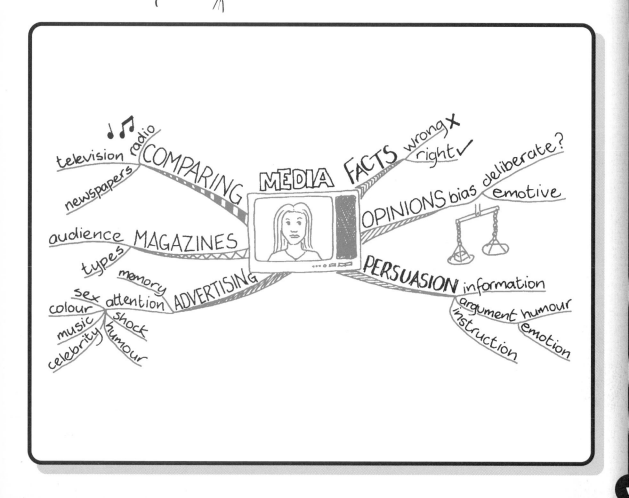

How to read a Mind Map

① Begin in the centre, the focus of your topic.

② The words/images attached to the centre are like chapter headings: read them next.

③ Always read out from the centre, in every direction (even on the left-hand side, where you will have to read from right to left, instead of the usual left to right).

How to draw a Mind Map

① Start in the middle of the page with the page turned sideways. This gives your brain the maximum width for its thoughts.

② Always start by drawing a small picture or symbol. Why? Because a picture is worth a thousand words to your brain. And try to use at least three colours, as colour helps your memory even more.

③ Write or draw your ideas on coloured branching lines connected to your central image. These key symbols and words are the headings for your topic.

④ Then add facts, further items and ideas by drawing more, smaller, branches on to the main branches, just like a tree.

⑤ Always print your word clearly on its line. Use only one word per line.

⑥ To link ideas and thoughts on different branches, use arrows, colours, underlining, and boxes.

Make life *easy* for your brain

When you start on a new book or topic there are several things you can do to help get your brain 'on line' faster:

① **Quickly scan through the whole book or topic,** as you would do if you were in a shop deciding whether or not to buy a book or magazine. This gives your brain *control*.

② **Think of what you already know about the subject.** You'll often find it's a lot more than you first thought. A good way of doing this is to do a quick Mind Map of *everything you know* about the subject after you have skimmed through it.

③ **Ask 'who?' 'what?' 'why?' 'where?' 'when?' and 'how?' questions about the topic.** Questions help your brain fish the knowledge out.

④ **Have another quick scan through.** Look at the diagrams, pictures and illustrations, and also at the beginnings and ends of sections – often most information is contained at the beginnings and ends.

⑤ **Build up a Mind Map.** This helps your brain to organise and remember information as you go.

⑥ **Mark up any difficult bits and move on.** Your brain *will* be able to solve the problems when you come back to them a little while later – much like saving the difficult bits of a jigsaw puzzle till last. They all fall into place in the end.

⑦ **Have a final scan.** Look through the book or topic quickly one more time. This will lodge it permanently in your memory banks.

And finally...

① *Have fun while you learn* – people who enjoy what they are doing understand and remember it more.

② *Use your teachers* as resource centres. Ask them for help with specific topics and with more general advice on how you can improve your all-round performance.

③ *Personalise your* **Success at Key Stage 3 English** by underlining and highlighting, by adding notes and pictures. Allow your brain to have a conversation with it!

Your brain is an amazing piece of equipment. The more you understand and use it, the more it will repay you. I wish you and your brain every success.

Tony Buzan

GCSE Revision guides from Teach Yourself

If you have enjoyed using this book at Key Stage 3, you might like to know about the range of Teach Yourself GCSE revision guides available from your local bookshop.

Subject guides

Mathematics: Higher Level	0 340 68860 2
Mathematics: Intermediate Level	0 340 66383 9
English	0 340 70159 5
Modern World History	0 340 66385 5
Geography	0 340 66386 3
French	0 340 66393 6
French cassette	0 340 70475 6
French book/cassette pack	0 340 70476 4
German	0 340 71145 0
German cassette	0 340 71147 7
German book/cassette pack	0 340 71146 9
Spanish	0 340 66389 8
Spanish cassette	0 340 70477 2
Spanish book/cassette pack	0 340 70478 0
Science: Double Award	0 340 66388 X
Science: Single Award	0 340 66387 1
Biology	0 340 66391 X
Chemistry	0 340 66392 8
Physics	0 340 66390 1
Information Technology	0 340 66384 7

Literature guides

Romeo and Juliet	0 340 66398 7
A Midsummer Night's Dream	0 340 66396 0
The Merchant of Venice	0 340 66395 2
Julius Caesar	0 340 68834 3
Macbeth	0 340 66397 9
Pride and Prejudice	0 340 67961 1
Wuthering Heights	0 340 69707 5
Great Expectations	0 340 66394 4
Far from the Madding Crowd	0 340 66404 5
A Portrait of the Artist as a Young Man	0 340 67960 3
Of Mice and Men	0 340 66402 9
Animal Farm	0 340 66401 0
Lord of the Flies	0 340 66400 2
To Kill a Mockingbird	0 340 66403 7
The Owl Service	0 340 67959 X

Key to symbols

As you read through this revision guide, you will notice symbols which occur frequently throughout the book. These are to help you identify specific sections of text quickly and easily while you revise. This is what they mean:

 Speaking and listening skills are needed (see p.10).

 Reading skills are needed (see p. 17).

 Section round-up: End-of-section reviews and revision tips.

 Writing skills are needed (see p. 10).

 Questions to answer to help with your revision, based on the section you have just read. These are typical of SATs questions.

 A good place to take a five- to ten-minute break.

 Ask yourself questions to help you to understand passages of writing.

 Checklist of topics covered in the chapter.

Speaking and listening

overview

This chapter is about enjoying, understanding and using spoken English. You will learn about:

- Accent, dialect and standard English.

- Changing your style of speech to fit the situation.

- Improving your speaking and listening skills.

Accent, dialect and standard English

about this section

This section explains why accents and dialects exist, and what they are. It also tells you what 'standard English' is, and when you should use it.

Origins of English

The English language changes all the time. Sometimes words change meaning. The word *sad* once meant 'full', then 'serious', then 'unhappy'. ✪ How do you use it? In addition, new words are introduced. Some come from other languages – such as *pyjamas*, from Urdu. Others are invented for new technologies – such as *rocket* and *download*.

If you could wave a magic wand and travel back in time a thousand years, you would find most people in England speaking Old English – also called Anglo-Saxon. There's a sample at the top of the next column.

I mycel englisc boc be gehwilcum thingum on leothwisan geworht.

This means: 'One big English book about all sorts of things, made in the style of a song'.

The Anglo-Saxons were just one group of invaders who settled in England. There were also Vikings in the north, then Normans spreading from the south after 1066. Their languages got mixed up into early English, like ingredients in a witch's cauldron. But they never completely blended. This is the main reason why we have **accents** and **dialects** in different areas.

Accents

Accents includes two things:
- **pronunciation** – for example, a Scot might pronounce *food* to rhyme with *could*;
- **intonation** – the musical rise and fall of the voice.

An accent from a particular area is called a **regional** accent. People from other countries also speak English with their own accents.

Dialects

A **dialect** is a particular style of English used in one area, or by speakers of English in other countries, or whose parents come from other countries. Dialects differ from standard English in two ways:

- **grammar** – differences in word order, and the use of pronouns and verbs (see page 138).
- **vocabulary** – individual words, such as the northern adjective *mardy* to describe a child who is whining and spoilt.

Dialects make English livelier and more interesting. Below is the start of a poem in the Trinidad dialect. Notice words suggesting accent, such as *meh* and *yuh* for 'my' and 'your', as well as dialect phrases which are different from standard English.

Granny in de Market Place (Amryl Johnson)

Yuh fish fresh?

Woman, why yuh holdin' meh fish up tuh yuh nose?
De fish fresh. Ah say it fresh. Ah ehn go say it any mo'

Hmmm, well if dis fish fresh den is I who dead an' gone
De ting smell like it take a bath in a lavatory in town
It here so long it happy. Look how de mout' laughin' at we
De eye turn up to heaven like it want tuh know 'e fate
Dey say it does take a good week before dey reach dat state

Standard English

Standard English is the most widely understood style of English. It is used by people who want to be easily understood by English speakers everywhere – such as newsreaders, politicians and those in business. It can be spoken in any accent. There is nothing wrong with speaking in a dialect, but sometimes – for example, in interviews – you need to speak in standard English.

This is yer news tonight. The Prime Minister's decided to chuck it all in,'cos he's fed up with people having a go at him. He's asked the Deputy Prime Minister to do the honours for a bit while the party gets an election sorted. The Leader of the House of Commons said, 'He's a great bloke. I'll be gutted to see him go.'

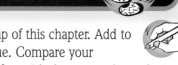

Task time

- Start a Mind Map of this chapter. Add to it as you continue. Compare your growing Mind Map with the one at the end.

- Make a local phrasebook for visitors to your area.

- Rewrite the newsreader's words above in standard English. Then write a sentence explaining to her why the news should be read in standard English. (Answers on page 14.)

- Read the extract from Amryl Johnson's poem aloud in a suitable accent. Underline the phrases that are different in grammar from standard English.

section round-up

By now you should know about:
- **The ingredients of early English.**
- **Accents and dialects.**
- **Standard English and when to use it.**

 Take a break before racing into 'register'.

Getting the right register

about this section

This section tells you about changing your style of speech to suit different situations.

Register

The way we speak varies according to three things:

- **Who** we are speaking to;
- **What** we are speaking about;
- **Why** we are speaking.

✪ How would you greet your headteacher? A close friend? A shop assistant? You would probably use different words and a different tone of voice each time. Now imagine you are:

- Apologising to your headteacher for breaking a window.
- Trying to cheer up a close friend whose pet has died.
- Complaining to a shop assistant that something you've bought has injured you.

✪ Try each of these out to see how your style of speech varies. The way in which you speak in different situations is called the **register**. Good speakers vary the register to suit the situation.

Quick check

❓ Make a Mini Mind Map showing the three factors that decide what register to use in a situation. (Keywords: Who, What, Why.) Add to it some of the different people, subjects and reasons for speaking that affect your register in a typical day.

WIZARD TIP
Formality

One important factor deciding what register to use is how **formal** a situation is. An interview is formal; a party or a chat with friends is **informal**. In formal situations, use standard English (see previous section), without slang or dialect. You should also avoid **colloquial** words and phrases – such as *kid* for 'child', or *hang about* for 'wait'.

Good afternoon, David. I have been intending to telephone you. My friends and I are having a social gathering with light refreshments at my house this evening. I would be delighted if you could attend.

'It would be excellent if I could come to your school. What it is, see, is that I live down the road, so I could pop back to grab some food at lunchtime. I've got loads of mates here, and I've heard that your exam results are really cool.

❓ Speaking aloud, reword the speech bubbles above in a more suitable register.

section round-up

'Register' is the style of speech we use in a particular situation. Things that decide it are: who we are speaking to, what we are saying and why we are saying it. We should speak formally in formal situations.

 Take a break before learning about listening.

1

Speaking and listening skills

about this section

This section is about developing your skills. It will tell you how to:
- listen more effectively
- have better conversations
- interview people
- speak effectively
- give a talk.

Listening

Try this. Close your eyes and just listen for about a minute – starting now. When you open your eyes again, note down what you could hear.

We get used to ignoring noise. You might even be reading this with the television or radio on, or with people talking in the background. Ignoring sounds is a useful skill, but there are times when we want to listen closely. Some possible distractions are shown in the illustration.

Listening tips

Listening is at least as important as talking. Here are some tips.

- Notice 'body language'. Is the person to whom you are talking shifting about nervously, slumping miserably, leaning back relaxed, or perhaps sitting up, arms folded – expecting an argument?
- Show that you are listening. Sit forward, don't glance about or stare out of the window. Comment occasionally: 'That must have been difficult!'; 'Right'; 'I see what you mean'.
- Ask questions: 'Hang on – who said that?'; 'So what did Lisa do then?'
- If given instructions, repeat them: 'OK. So, I go left past the ice rink ...'

- In groups, try to get an overview of the way the discussion is going, as well as listening to individuals. If there's something you feel you must say, but someone's speaking, jot down a keyword reminder.

Talks and teachers

If you're listening to a talk, or to a teacher speaking at length, make brief keyword notes or a Mini Mind Map. This will keep you alert and give you a useful reminder for later.

Telephones

Telephone conversations are different from face-to-face conversations. You can't see body language or facial expressions, or make eye contact. Making keyword notes or a Mind Map can really help. For an important call you could do this beforehand. You can also jot down keywords reminders during the conversation.

'I wonder what's for tea.......Oh, so he knows Sharon. I've got a book of hers–must give it back.......'

'I hope she doesn't think I'm stupid....... What can I say if there's an embarrassing silence? Is that Wayne over there?'

Interviews

Your schoolwork may involve interviewing someone – perhaps a fellow student or a relative at home. Here are some tips.

- Give your interviewee some idea of what you need to know before you start.
- Prepare a list of questions, but be flexible. If your interviewee starts to talk about something interesting and useful, you may want to find out more about that.
- 'Open' questions are often more useful than 'closed' questions. An open question is one that could have all sorts of answers: 'How did you feel?' Closed questions invite yes/no answers: 'Did you feel excited?'

Speaking and giving a talk

To speak effectively, try to put yourself in the shoes of your listeners. Do you need to explain anything or use simpler language? Will they be interested? Have you got their attention? Try to speak in a lively way, putting expression into what you say.

Giving a talk to the class or in public can be scary, but there are some simple hints that will make it much easier for you and more enjoyable for your audience.

- Plan your talk using a large Mind Map. Use different colours for the branches and number them in order. This is much easier than using ordinary notes or cards.
- Work out how long to spend on each part of the talk. If using a Mind Map, you will be able to see the whole plan at a glance and make changes easily if you run short of time.
- Use the 1-2-3 system: (1) Say what you plan to say; (2) Say it; (3) Say what you've said!
- Take deep breaths to calm down. Look at people in the audience as you speak. Don't gabble! Nervous speakers often go so fast no one can follow them.

Practice time

? Listen to the radio news. Make keyword notes or a Mini Mind Map. Then tell a friend or parent the news. Make it interesting!

? Work with a friend. Take it in turns to spend two minutes telling the other person about an event in your life. The other person should listen silently, then try to tell you about it as accurately as possible.

? Make a Mind Map for a talk on your favourite hobby. Practise giving the talk to an adult. Remember the 1-2-3 system.

? Watch television interviews. Notice the techniques interviewers use to keep guests talking interestingly.

section round-up

This section has told you how to help yourself to listen, given you hints on interviewing and told you how to speak effectively. It has also told you how to prepare and give a talk. If you find you can now tell a friend all about it, well done!

Spell-binding
To work some memory magic, remind yourself now of what you've learnt. If you've been making a chapter Mind Map, check it against the Mind Map on page 14. Then try the checklist.

1

checklist

Could you now:

	Yes	Not yet

1 Explain the difference between accent and dialect? (p. 9–10)

2 Say what standard English is and when you need to use it? (p. 10)

3 Comment on how different registers suit different situations? (p. 11)

4 Think of two ways to improve your listening skills? (p. 12)

5 Explain what 'open' and 'closed' questions are? (p. 13)

6 Plan a talk? (p. 13)

If your answer to any of these questions is 'Not yet', look back at the pages shown. If you're still unsure, ask your teacher for help.

Answers

(page 10): This is the news tonight. The Prime Minister has decided to resign, because he is tired of people criticising him. He has asked the Deputy Prime Minister to take over for a short time while the party organises an election. The Leader of the House of Commons said, 'He's a very nice man. I'll be very sorry to see him go.'
She should use standard English so that people understand her easily and respect what she says.

Reading

overview

Reading is something you do so often and so automatically that you probably never stop to think about how and why you read. All day you are taking in written words: signs and posters, advertising hoardings, leaflets, instructions and information on your computer, textbooks in school. You read the menu in the school dining hall, you read notices about clubs and activities. This chapter will teach you about:

- Different reasons for reading.

- Different ways of reading.

- Taking notes on what you read.

- Developing your own reading habits.

- Keeping track of your own reading.

Reading for a reason

about this section

This section focuses on the different reasons we have for reading.

Different purposes

Your reasons for reading a story or a novel are different from your reasons for reading a letter about a parent–teacher evening or a notice about a sports event.

Try this

Who might read each of the examples below? What would be their reason for reading it? Write your answers in the boxes.

A

> I was in the cinema queue when the fight started. I saw a black Ford Escort drive up. The time was about 7:15. Three men jumped out of the car and ran to the end of the building. I heard a lot of noise and looked round to see what was going on.

Who
Reason for reading

B

> **Ingredients**
> 1 tablespoon of oil
> 1 onion, chopped
> 2 celery sticks, sliced
> 1 red pepper, cored and seeded

Who
Reason for reading

C

> At eight o'clock the baby started to cry. Jo sighed and put down her pen. Just her luck to be saddled with a crying baby when she'd counted on an evening's work without interruptions.

Who
Reason for reading

D

BBC1	BBC2	ITV
4.35 The Mask	4.25 Ready Steady	4.20 Mike and Angelo
5.00 Newsround	Cook	4.45 Sharp Practice
5.10 The Demon	4.55 Esther	5.10 Home and Away
Headmaster	5.30 Today's the Day	

Who	
Reason for reading	

E

read (riːd) 1. to comprehend the meaning of something (written or printed) by looking at and interpreting the written and printed characters.

Who	
Reason for reading	

The activity above has helped you to identify some of the main reasons for reading. We read to find out things we need to know to help us to perform tasks and go about our daily lives. We read to get information. We read to find out facts. We also read to discover other people's ideas about human beings and the world we live in. We read for pleasure and entertainment.

Some of these ideas and others dealt with in this chapter are shown in the Mind Map. Add to it as you work through the chapter. You could include examples and references from your own reading.

section round-up

You've learnt that reading is done for different purposes and have identified some of the reasons.

Have a break before skimming ahead.

Skimming, scanning and note-making

Skimming the surface

Skimming is a reading method that helps you to grasp the meaning of a piece of writing quickly. When you read like this you are not trying to pick up the details in the passage, but to get a rough idea of what it's about. You are getting a quick preview of the material. Follow these four simple steps:

1 Know **why** you are reading the text. Is it to get information that you want to use, or that you will have to remember? Will you need to select certain facts? Is it to enjoy and understand a novel or story?

2 Know **what** the reading matter is about. Titles and headings will help you – the book title, the chapter title, the section heading, the contents page, the index, the writing on the front or back of the book, the introduction to the book or extract.

3 As you skim through the material, ask yourself questions. What is this about? Who is this about? What seems to be happening?

4 Test yourself. Can you give somebody else a rough idea of what the text is about?

Try to skim at the rate of 10 seconds per page. Use a guide such as a thin pen, or a chopstick, to point.

Have a go

Practise by skim-reading this book. Follow the four steps above, then see if you can answer these questions.

How many chapters does this book have?

Does it contain material about Shakespeare; the Bible; fiction written before 1900?

On which pages would you find information about advertising; drafting; diaries?

Does the book contain material about Chinese literature?

Some of the text is in boxes. Which character introduces these boxes? What are they for?

Smart scanning

Another kind of reading is called **scanning**. This is what you do when you want to find out particular bits of information. You don't read every word, but you run your eye over the page until you find what you need. You know what you are looking for and are scanning the text for key words and phrases.

✪ What other situations can you add to the list of where you would use the technique of scanning?

- looking in the cupboard for your favourite cereal
- looking for a number in the telephone directory
- finding a road on a road map.

2

? Read through these extracts from a holiday brochure. You are looking for a hotel that takes pets and is close to a surfing beach. Put a cross or a tick in the balloons in the illustration to show which you have chosen.

CRANFORD HOTEL

1 Sea Street, Seatown

A family-run hotel for 30 years, with 20 en-suite rooms and three spacious family rooms. We offer babysitting facilities and can provide early evening meals for youngsters if you wish. Pets welcome. We have a gourmet restaurant and a well-stocked bar. Cable TV in all rooms. Beaches for all the family within a few minutes' walk. Beaches for swimmers and surfers just a little further along the front. Reduced admission to Leisure Centre for guests staying for a week or longer.

SEA VIEW

8 Shore Road, Seatown

Comfortable hotel with a family atmosphere. All rooms en-suite with colour TV and tea-making facilities. Our friendly restaurant is open all day. Meals available at set times; snacks (toasties, sandwiches, selection of pastries) available at all times. Central heating; just six minutes walk to the city centre and three minutes to family and surfing beaches. Games room and bar on lower ground floor. Children and pets welcome. Weekly theme banquet (Mexican, Indian, Olde English).

SEA PARADISE

6 The Parade, Seatown

If sporting and surfing's your bag, get on down to Sea Paradise! If we were closer to the sea we'd be in it. Just roll out of your bed in your comfortable en-suite room, grab a bite in our open-all-hours bar and you'll be riding the waves before you can say Hawaii. Cable in all rooms; wide screen in our lively Sports Bar. Leave the kids and parents at home – oh, and sorry you pooches, we can't take pets right now. We fill up pretty quickly, so book your accommodation soonest!

Nifty notes

Taking notes on what you read is an essential skill. There are many methods of note-taking, and you may already be using a particular technique in English and in your other subjects. Some types of note-taking are likely to be more effective than others, so make sure that your method makes the best possible use of your brain power. If you haven't already done so, turn to the front of the book and read about how to use Mind Maps.

Why make notes?

When you read it's important to identify the main points in the text and to remember them. If you make effective notes you will be able to recall the material without re-reading every word of the book.

What kind of notes should I make?

Mind Mapping is the smartest way to make notes. Whatever technique you choose, here are six rules you will find helpful:

1 Group main ideas.
2 Leave out any word that is unnecessary.
3 Use signs instead of words.
4 Use bullet points rather than sentences.
5 Use colour.
6 Use arrows to link ideas.

WIZARD WAY WITH NOTES

A way to make totally personal customised notes (which can still be understood by others) is to use **colour** and **pictures**. You can use colour in different ways – to show that ideas are linked, to emphasise the most important words, to identify characters. ✪ For what kind of character might you use fiery red? For what kind of character might you use cool blue? Or sad blue? Who might be shown as threatening black? Have some fun!

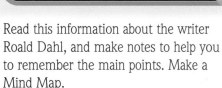

Try this

Read this information about the writer Roald Dahl, and make notes to help you to remember the main points. Make a Mind Map.

The popular children's writer Roald Dahl was born in Wales in 1916 and educated at Repton School, Yorkshire. During the Second World War (1939–45) he was a fighter-pilot in the Royal Air Force. In 1953 he married the actress Patricia Neal and the couple had one son and four daughters, one of whom sadly died. In 1983 the couple divorced and Dahl married Felicity Crosland.

Roald Dahl used to make up bedtime stories for his children, and one of the stories became *James and the Giant Peach*, published in 1961. This was followed by favourites such as *Charlie and the Chocolate Factory, Danny the Champion of the World* and *The Wonderful Story of Henry Sugar*. Among his most popular works are *The Twits, Matilda* and *The Witches*.

Some adults dislike Roald Dahl's children's books because they are cruel and nasty. For example, in *George's Marvellous Medicine*, George gives his horrible grandmother some medicine that does dreadful things to her. However, millions of children love his books. ✪ What do you think?

section round-up

If you've worked your way through this section you should be clear about two different reading methods, and have some ideas about how to make effective notes. Well done.

2

What to read

about this section

Whether you are already a keen reader or just getting going with your own reading choices, it can sometimes be difficult to know what to read. With all the thousands of books available, how do you know where to start? Have you ever felt that you'd like a change from the kind of book that you've been reading, but don't know what else to choose, so end up with another from the same series? Don't worry – help is at hand. This section will give you ideas about choosing books that you will enjoy and that will help you to read more widely.

What do you read?

Even if you wouldn't describe yourself as a reader, you will certainly read a great deal during the course of a school day! On the whole, what you read in school isn't your own independent choice. You will improve every aspect of your work in English if you choose a range of fiction and non-fiction to read – and you will develop a lifelong habit that will bring you great enjoyment!

✪ What have you read this year? Fill in the chart.

✪ What does the chart tell you about your reading habits? Decide now to extend your reading by branching out into something different.

Type of book	Title(s)	Enjoyment rating *(least) > *****(most)
horror fiction		
fantasy fiction		
romance		
family fiction	Goggle Eyes by Ann Fine	***** – I'll read her other books now
historical fiction		
thrillers/adventure stories		
detective fiction		
travel writing		
people's lives		
information for projects		
information for enjoyment		
plays		
poetry		
comics/magazines		

Which one to choose?

Use the **skimming** technique that you practised in the last section. Read the title, look at what is written on the front and back cover and skim through the pages. Glance at chapter headings, at the amount of dialogue, at bits of paragraphs. If it catches your interest, go ahead.

 Read these extracts from some first pages of novels. Which of them interests you most? Put them in order of interest. Swap ideas with a friend.

A

Beyond Claypole Ridge there is Ogdentown, about ten miles further. But there is no one left alive in Ogdentown.

B

As Gregor Samsa awoke one morning from uneasy dreams he found himself transformed in his bed into a giant insect.

C

Lyra and her demon moved through the darkening Hall, taking care to keep to one side, out of sight of the kitchen.

D

Five miles outside Glastonbury.
2.58 am
Brindled with bitter, biting frost, the plough-churned soil of the Somerset levels was bare and black.

E

Edith walked into the classroom at late morning, causing the teacher to stop in the middle of one of her monotonous sentences to fasten a hate-filled glare, which Edith never saw, on her back.

F

East and West, the sirens wailed. Emergency procedures began, hampered here and there by understandable panic. Helpful leaflets were distributed and roads sealed off. Suddenly, nobody wanted to be an engine-driver any more, or a model or a rock-star. Everybody wanted to be one thing: a survivor.

G

Somehow or other John had got himself into a hopeless mess. After tonight's row, after Sonia had stormed out of the flat for what he hoped was positively the very last time, he decided to sort it out.

What do you learn about the books from these extracts? You could discuss the setting, the characters, the period, the style.
Turn to the end of this chapter to discover the books' titles. You could decide to read one, or more, or even all – they are all different, and all are excellent!

Make a note of all the authors mentioned in this book. Write them in your own Wizard read box. Find out what other books they have written.

WIZARD READ

2

Where to get books

There are various places and people who could be good sources of books. The Mind Map shows some ideas – add your own!

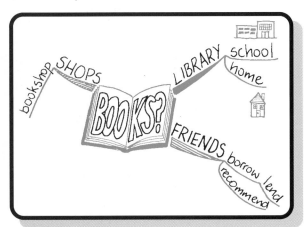

How to choose

Once you have decided what kind of book you want to read next, focus on authors. Some authors write particular kinds of books. For example, Joan Lingard writes books about families and teenagers in Northern Ireland, Nigel Hinton writes adventure and family stories about teenagers, Marjorie Darke writes historical fiction.

WIZARD TIP FOR CHOOSING BOOKS

Your local library can help. Many libraries have a database of titles and authors. All you do is type in either the kind of book you want, or an author's name, and you will get a list to choose from. Go on – if you haven't already used this facility, try it out! Your librarian will help you.

section round-up R

You should know how to go about widening your range of reading, and have some names and titles to look for.

STOP   Have a break before logging on.

The Mind Map gives you some more ideas for your own reading. Add your own titles and comments.

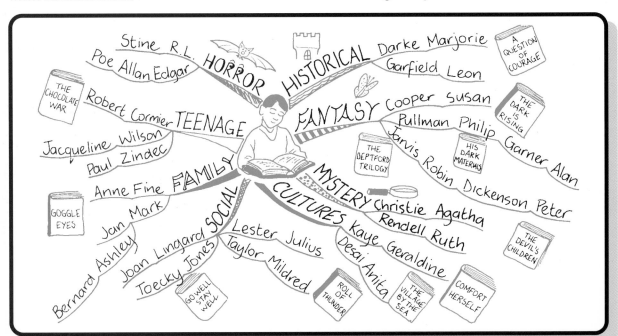

Keeping a reading diary

about this section

This section focuses on your reading diary, sometimes called a reading log. You will learn how useful it is to keep a reading diary, and you will get some ideas about what to write in the diary and how to write it.

Why keep a reading diary?

Keeping a reading diary is an excellent way of recording what you read and how you respond to what you read. It will provide you with a useful record, and will also help your teacher to assess your reading skills and how they are developing. Of course, your reading diary will do this only if you write helpful comments.

What should I write in it?

When you read a fictional work, you should comment on the setting, the characters, the language, the plot and the mood or feeling of the story. (There is more about this in Chapter 5.) Here are some useful questions to ask yourself as you read:

- Where and when is the story set? How important are the period and the location?
- Who are the main characters? What impression have you gained of each? How important is each character to the story?
- How is language used? Is there description, dialogue? Do you notice any effective use of language?

- What happens? Are there any unexpected events or twists? Is the plot less important than the characters?
- How does the story make you feel? Do your feelings change at different parts? Does your attitude to any of the characters change?

Winning entry

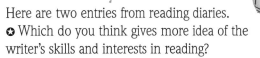

Here are two entries from reading diaries.
 Which do you think gives more idea of the writer's skills and interests in reading?

A

I thought 'Brother in the Land' was gripping and quite disturbing. The author made me feel the tensions between the different groups of people who had been lucky, or unlucky, to survive a nuclear attack. I thought the saddest bits were when the deformed baby was born and when they buried Ben.

B

'Brother in the Land' was the best book I've read this year. It took me a long time to get into it but then I enjoyed it. I would recommend it and give it ten out of ten.

2

WIZARD WAYS WITH YOUR READING DIARY

Here are some phrases that will help you to write about your chosen books:

My favourite character is........because..........

My feelings towards.......changed as the book went on. At the beginning.......

I thought that the book's language was.......

Try this

 Choose a book you have read recently and write about it on the chart below. Try to fill in every section.

? You could copy this chart, or make one to your own design.

TITLE

AUTHOR

DATE BEGUN   DATE FINISHED

PLOT

CHARACTERS

SETTING

WHAT I ENJOYED

WHAT I DIDN'T ENJOY

ANY OTHER COMMENTS

OTHER TITLES BY SAME AUTHOR

WHAT I WILL READ NEXT

section round-up

Now you know the benefits of keeping a reading diary and the kind of information to include in it.

SPELL-BINDING

To work some memory magic, remind yourself of what you've learnt. If you've been adding to a chapter Mind Map, review it now. Then try the checklist.

checklist

Could you now:

	Yes	Not yet
1 Name different reasons for reading? (p. 15)	◯	◯
2 Describe two reading techniques? (p. 17)	◯	◯
3 Explain how to make effective notes? (p. 19)	◯	◯
4 Decide how to choose what to read? (p. 20)	◯	◯
5 Keep a reading diary? (p. 23)	◯	◯

If your answer to any of these questions is 'Not yet', look back at the pages shown. If you're still unsure, ask your teacher for help.

Answers

(p. 12): Titles of books in 'Which one do I choose?'
A Z for Zachariah by Robert O'Brien
B Metamorphosis by Franz Kafka **C** Northern Lights by Philip Pullman **D** The Raven's Knot by Robin Jarvis **E** The Friends by Rosa Guy **F** Brother in the Land by Robert Swindells **G** Stung from A Sense of Shame by Jan Needle

Writing

overview

This chapter will make your written English better organised, clearer, more effective and more interesting. It covers:

- Writing for a particular purpose and audience.
- Planning.
- Beginnings and endings.
- Improving your style.

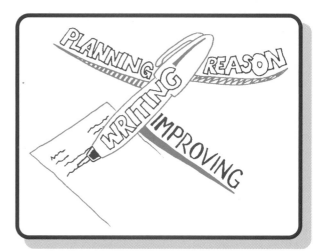

Writing for a reason

about this section

This section tells you how to write in a style to suit your purpose and audience.

Purpose

Whatever you write, you must understand its **purpose** – what it's for. Even if your main reason for writing is to keep out of trouble, you must think about the situations outside of school when a particular kind of writing might be needed.

The pictures below suggest some possible writing purposes. ✪ Try to guess what each one is.

Now read the examples below. They show writing for different purposes, starting with the purposes shown in the pictures above. Notice the differences in **style**.

Style

This good-looking mountain bike is built to withstand tough treatment, yet it weighs less than many road bikes. **To sell: emphasising the good points.**

To change the inner tube, first remove the wheel. Use a spanner to loosen both wheel-nuts. **To instruct: clear, step-by-step, straightforward.**

Always wear a helmet when rough-riding. Accidents do happen and head injuries can be dangerous. **To warn: stating clearly what you should do, and why.**

The chilly wind rushed through her hair, carrying away worries like smoke. As she neared the gate, she pulled at the brakes. Nothing! Just the click of metal, and the gate looming larger by the second. **To entertain – in this case by telling a story, bringing a situation to life.**

The first bicycle appeared in Paris in 1791. Now there are 800 million bicycles worldwide – twice as many as the number of cars. **To inform: gives facts in a straightforward way.**

Cycling is cheap, gets you fit and causes no pollution. The government should do all it can to encourage it. **To persuade: Gives arguments and conclusions.**

I'm only 8 but I'm a good reader. I like animals.

Sarah Sweet

I'm 14. I know a bit about most things, I've got wide interests.

Clara Clever

Nadim Normal

As it happens, I'm an expert on whatever you know most about.

Subject	Purpose
Dogs	Persuade
Your local area	Inform
Your favourite sport	Warn
Healthy eating	Entertain
Whatever you know most about	Sell

Audience

The people who read what you write are your **audience**. They could be young or old, male or female, rich or poor, experts or beginners. Think about what you read yourself: you are part of an audience. Remember, too, that your typical reader may be in a particular situation – on a plane, on holiday, or just about to go for a swim in shark-infested water!

WIZARD TIP

Try to write for an audience. Ask yourself what your audience needs to be told and in what style. You could ask a friend or parent to read your writing. Tell them its purpose, so they don't just look for mistakes!

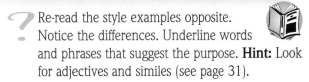
Write for a reason

Re-read the style examples opposite. Notice the differences. Underline words and phrases that suggest the purpose. **Hint:** Look for adjectives and similes (see page 31).

Try to match the following things a reader might say or think, with the reasons for writing that you've read about.

I want one!

Mmmm ... that's interesting

What's going to happen next?

I see your point, but I still think ...

Oh, so <u>that's</u> how you do it.

Ha ha ha!

Choose a reader, subject and purpose from the box on the left. Write a piece aimed at that reader, on that subject, and for that purpose.

Rewrite each of the following in a more suitable style:

Exercising in this area is inadvisable, owing to the presence of the carnivorous marine creature, *Carcharadon carcharias* (great white shark).

To keep your wheeled wonder racing like the wind, lovingly squeeze a few golden drops of oil on to the glistening black centipede that turns ever onward as you pedal.

section round-up

This section has told you how to fit your writing style to your purpose – for example to sell, to instruct or to warn. It has also told you about writing for a particular audience.

Take a break before making a plan.

Planning

about this section

This section is about planning, so that your writing has a structure which readers can follow, and so that you don't get stuck half-way. It covers:

- Descriptive accounts.

- Persuasive essays.

- Writing about literature.

- Your own stories.

Brainstorming

Begin your plan with **brainstorming** – letting yourself produce lots of different ideas about your subject. You will use some of the ideas and not others. Don't worry about waste: your brain is full of ideas! At this stage, don't judge your ideas or go into detail.

One way to brainstorm is to jot down ideas, scattered over a sheet of plain paper. You may find that you think better walking around, or even talking out loud! Brainstorming with a friend also works well.

Mind Mapping

Use a Mind Map to brainstorm. You can easily add to it, and your ideas start to turn into a plan almost like magic. When it's finished decide on the order in which to use your ideas. Number the branches in that order – and there's your plan! Here's an example:

Write about overcoming something you were afraid of.

When I heard that one of our school camp activities was caving, I wanted to find out more. I had been in show caves before and heard about 'adventure caving', and it sounded exciting. I hoped I would see stalagmites and stalactites. I think I also wanted to impress my friends, as well as having fun. I hoped I wouldn't be too scared. Most of all, I hoped I would survive!

I lay awake the night before, thinking about next day. We would be deep underground. Unlike the bats, we would be relying on electric caving lights. It might be quite hard as well – and I'm not very sporty. But my biggest fear was **claustrophobia** – fear of small spaces. When I was small, my sister shut me in a wardrobe. I was terrified.

In the morning we all piled into the big white van. There were ten of us, along with Miss Dobbs and the caving instructor, called Phil. Most of us were a bit noisy. Dan was very quiet, and his face seemed to be turning pale green, like mould. I talked a lot, because of nerves. I tried to cheer Dan up: 'Come on, your dad was a miner!' It took my mind off things.

After an hour we came to a halt. We got out and Phil gave us plastic oversuits, belts, batteries with lights and helmets to put on. My fingers were turning to jelly. I had to get Miss Dobbs to help do my belt up. In a few minutes, we set off, with Dan at the back.

The cave was across three fields. When Phil showed us the entrance I laughed. Then, with horror, I realised that he wasn't joking. It was like a rabbit hole with a muddy stream rushing into it.

I went in third. I was wet within seconds, though the oversuit kept out most of the water. We had to crawl in the stream at first, and it seemed like I'd never be able to turn around. Then, after about five minutes we could stand up. Then came more stream passage, a few slippery climbs up and down piles of rocks, a tight squeeze, and then a chamber dripping with stalagmites and stalactites. We all helped each other and that made it more fun. An hour and a half later, we turned round to come back. I wanted to go on. I wasn't scared anymore! In fact, I wondered why I ever had been.

Later, after a shower and supper, I thought about our caving trip. Next time I won't be scared. I suppose things you don't know about are often scary – then they turn out to be all right after all.

Persuasive essays

A persuasive essay must give arguments to support your point of view. Again, Mind Mapping is a good planning technique. Try to order your ideas so that they run on naturally from each other. A general plan to follow is:

1 Introduce the question or problem.
2 Your evidence and arguments.
3 Counter-arguments and why you disagree with them.
4 Your conclusions.

Writing about a character

You will often be asked to write about a character in a novel or play. Your technique should be similar to

the one for 'Persuasive essays', but there are some special things to consider.

- How the character is described. Look especially at the character's first appearance.
- What the character says and does.
- The character's relationship with other characters.
- Evidence to back up what you say, in the form of short quotations or examples.

Writing your own stories

The basic ingredients of a story, and some of the options, are shown in the Mind Map below. Some people find it easiest to think of characters first (who), then where they are (setting), then what they do (storyline). See what works for you. If you plan these things, you'll write faster and more effectively.

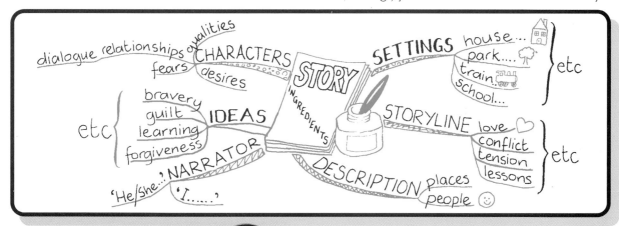

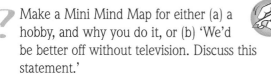
Planning practice

 Compare the caving account with the Mind Map. How closely did the student stick to the plan?

Make a Mini Mind Map for either (a) a hobby, and why you do it, or (b) 'We'd be better off without television. Discuss this statement.'

Plan a story of your own, using the 'ingredients' Mind Map.

With a friend, brainstorm ideas about a character in a novel or play you have both read.

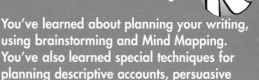
section round-up

You've learned about planning your writing, using brainstorming and Mind Mapping. You've also learned special techniques for planning descriptive accounts, persuasive and character essays, and your own stories.

 Now take a break!

Improving your writing

Beginnings

It is easier to start a piece of writing if you have planned it properly. You also need to know how you want it to end. For example, if you're writing a 'Whodunnit?', you will need to know who dunnit yourself, so that you can drop clues as you go along.

In non-fiction you need to do two things in the first few sentences:

- get the reader interested
- give the reader a clear idea of what the piece of writing is about.

News stories must give the basic information immediately. For example:

> A boy of 14 was last night rescued, unharmed, from a burning building in Chard.

With descriptive accounts you can be more flexible. Look again at the opening to the student essay in the previous section:

> When I heard that one of our school camp activities was caving, I wanted to find out more.

This gives just enough information to get us involved. We know now that the author is a pupil on a school camp, who has probably not been caving before but is interested. We can guess that the piece will be about caving and we start to become curious.

This account could have begun in lots of ways. Compare:

> 'Right, everyone,' called out Miss Dobbs, clapping her hands for attention. 'We've got a new activity on the list – caving. We can take ten of you ...'

or

> When I was 5, my sister shut me in a wardrobe. I was terrified. So when I had a chance to go caving on a school camp ...'

✪ Which do you think works best?

In fiction there is less need to give the basic information straight away and more need to arouse interest. Look at these short story beginnings. ✪ Ask yourself what information each one gives, what questions it makes you ask, and whether it makes you want to read on.

> *It was the night before the day fixed for his coronation, and the young King was sitting alone in his beautiful chamber.*
> *(Oscar Wilde,* The Young King*)*

> *The small locomotive engine, Number 4, came clanking, stumbling down from Selston with seven full wagons.*
> *(D. H. Lawrence,* Odour of Chrysanthemums*)*

> *To the eyes of a man viewing it from behind, the nut-brown hair was a wonder and a mystery.*
> *(Thomas Hardy,* The Son's Veto*)*

Endings

It is important to make your reader feel that you have come to a real conclusion, and not just run out of time or energy. Here, again, is the ending to the essay from the previous section:

> Next time I won't be scared. I suppose things you don't know about are often scary – then they turn out to be all right after all.

This looks forward to the future and shows a lesson learned: that our fears of the unknown usually prove to be unnecessary.

Another way to end is to echo the beginning. You can do this by taking the reader back to the character or scene with which you started. For example, an essay about school life that began with a description of a crowded classroom could end:

> Room 35 is quiet now, except for the tapping of the cleaner's broom against the desks. The caretaker walks past whistling. No more kids until tomorrow.

Improving your writing style

Good English is partly a matter of good grammar. Chapter 11 will help you with this. However, it also means good **style**. This means choosing words well and making your writing lively and easy to read. The more good writing you read, the better your own style will become.

Description

A story is more than just an account of what happens. To make it come alive, you must describe characters and scenes, and make your reader see what <u>you</u> can see in your imagination:

> Her dark eyes moved restlessly around, and her small fingers tapped on the table with a fidgety nervousness.

> Dirty white cliffs rose out of the choppy grey sea. Above, they jutted out of the land like a jawline from a face.

In fiction use **adjectives** (e.g. *dark*, *small*), **adverbs** (*restlessly*) and **similes** (*like a jawline out of a face*). Use them less often in non-fiction.

Smooth flow

You can check that your writing flows smoothly by reading it aloud. Sometimes you will want to use short sentences for effect – for example, to create suspense. At other times, link words are very useful:

and   because   or   but   although   which   who   despite   however

Repetition

You may sometimes want to repeat a word for effect. For example: 'She was quick to anger, quick to take offence, and quick to forgive.' More often, it is better to avoid repetition by thinking of different words to use. A dictionary or a thesaurus may help you to do this.

Do some word magic

? Read the openings of three novels or short stories. Make notes or Mini Mind Maps on (a) the information they give, and (b) the questions they make you ask.

? Write two beginnings of your own to the caving account.

? Continue one of the short story openings from this section in your own words for at least two more sentences. Try to follow the style used by the author.

? Write different endings to three of your own essays or stories.

? Add adjectives, adverbs and a simile to this sentence:

> The boy ran down the pitch, avoiding three defenders, and before the crowd knew what was happening the ball was speeding through the goalkeeper's legs like ...

3

? Turn the following into two smooth sentences by using link words:

> I got up. I had some breakfast. I wasn't hungry. I needed to lose weight. Today wasn't a good day to start. I was running in the London marathon.

? Write down as many words as you can to replace *beautiful*, *horrible* and *big*.

section round-up

You have been learning how to write more effectively and interestingly. This involves:
- Beginnings that give basic information and arouse interest.
- Endings that round off a piece of writing.
- Using descriptive words and link words.
- Avoiding repetition.

SPELL-BINDING

To work some memory magic, remind yourself now of what you've learnt. If you've been making a chapter Mind Map, check it against the Mind Map on this page. Then try the checklist.

checklist

Could you now:

	Yes	Not yet
1 Name three different writing purposes? (p. 26)	◯	◯
2 Write for a purpose and audience (e.g. to entertain friends)? (p. 27)	◯	◯
3 Use Mind Mapping to plan an essay or short story? (p. 28)	◯	◯
4 Write good beginnings and endings? (pp. 30–1)	◯	◯
5 Write a good description of a place or person? (p. 31)	◯	◯
6 Use link words and begin to avoid repetitions? (p. 31)	◯	◯

If your answer to any of these questions is 'Not yet', look back at the pages shown. If you're still unsure, ask your teacher for help.

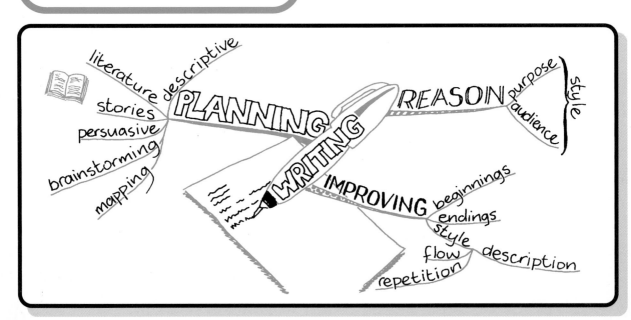

In the beginning

overview

This chapter is about the beginnings of English literature. It includes:

- Myths – the earliest stories of the gods.

- Legends – ancient stories based on real people and events.

- Epic tales of perilous missions.

- Early influences – the Bible and Chaucer.

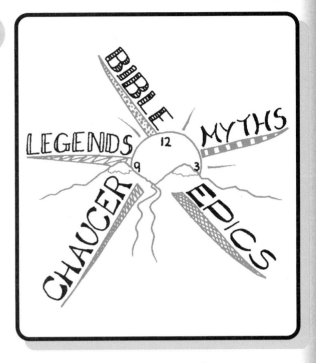

Myths

about this section

This section explains why myths are important in English literature.

Long before writing was invented, there were myths. These were stories going back further than anyone could possibly remember, passed down by word of mouth and changing a little each time they were told. They were about gods and humans, magical beasts, good and evil. Many myths explain in some way why the world is as it is.

The myths of the ancient Greeks play a big part in English literature. Many English writers have written about them, especially about the gods. Here are some of the main gods:

WORD MAGIC

Hermes was the only god able to pass between the land of the living and Hades – the land of the dead. It was he who guided souls into Hades. In this role, he was known as a *psychopomp*. The Greek word *psyche* means 'soul'. ✪ What other words do you know beginning with *psycho*?

Greek name	Roman name	Role
Zeus	Jupiter	Father of the gods, god of wisdom
Hera	Juno	Wife of Zeus, goddess of marriage and home
Ares	Mars	God of war
Aphrodite	Venus	Goddess of love and beauty
Hades	Pluto	God of death and the Underworld
Poseidon	Neptune	God of the sea
Hermes	Mercury	Winged messenger of the gods, god of thieves

The God of Thieves

Even as a very young child, Hermes loved to make mischief. One good way to do this was to steal what didn't belong to him. Once, he decided to steal 50 cows belonging to his older brother, the great god Apollo. He drove them by night, making them walk backwards so that anyone seeing their hoofprints would think they were heading in the opposite direction. He disguised his own tracks by wearing huge sandals made of tamarisk branches and myrtle twigs.

The child-god hid the cows in a cave. Then he set about making a roaring fire and roasted two of them. Next he divided the meat into 12 portions – one for each god and not forgetting himself, of course. He felt sure that if he was found out the gods would quickly forgive him once he offered them their portion of beef. Happy with his work, he went home and tucked himself up in his cradle.

Apollo soon discovered that 50 of his cows were missing. He was furious and he had a good idea who the culprit was. Of course, Hermes denied everything. Apollo carried him off to Zeus. The father of the gods laughed long and loud, but eventually he made Hermes take Apollo to the cave where the cows were hidden.

Apollo was still not satisfied, but Hermes had a peace offering for him: a lyre – a musical instrument that Hermes had just invented, made from a tortoise shell. Apollo was delighted and forgave Hermes. They became good friends. What's more, Apollo learnt to play the lyre and became god of music. Hermes became the protector of cattle – and the god of thieves.

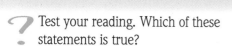

Task time

? Test your reading. Which of these statements is true?

1. Hermes is Apollo's younger brother.
2. Zeus lets Hermes keep the cows.
3. Hermes roasts two tortoises.
4. Hermes invents the lyre.

? Begin a Mind Map of this chapter. Add to it as you go work through these pages. Compare your Mind Map with the full Mind Map at the end of the chapter.

? The Greek and Roman god names are often used by companies. Look them up in the business pages of the telephone directory. Make notes of any that you find.

? Write out a short dialogue (conversation) that might take place when Apollo accuses Hermes.

section round-up

You should now be able to explain what a myth is and name some of the gods in the Greek myths. You should also be able to say why myths are important in English literature.

Take a break before leaping into legends.

Legends

What are legends?

The word **legend** is often used for someone who has become special in the imaginations of ordinary people – such as Marilyn Monroe or Muhammad Ali. Here we will look at the earlier type of **legend**: an old story that was originally about real people, but which has changed over the years in being told, so that we can no longer be certain how much of it really happened.

King Arthur

Many people believe that King Arthur was a Celtic king of Britain who fought the Saxons. Part of his legend is that he and his knights lie sleeping somewhere underground and that they will awake when Britain needs them. Now read the story below.

KING ARTHUR, GAWAIN AND LADY RAGNELL

Arthur was a wise king. Yet one Christmas, he was tricked into helping a young woman who came pleading to him. She claimed her husband had been taken prisoner by the wicked Knight of Tarn Wathelyne.

Arthur's knights begged him to let one of them go in his place, but he was not to be persuaded. He took his sword, Excalibur, and rode off with the young woman. When he reached the dark and towering castle, he found a huge and terrible figure on horseback standing solidly on the castle drawbridge.

'Is that Arthur, miserable monarch and cowardly king?' taunted the Knight of Tarn Wathelyne.

Arthur was so angry, he charged at the knight there and then. Down the road his horse pounded – but only to stop dead, whinnying in terror on the drawbridge. Arthur was gripped by a strange fear. His arms hung useless by his side. He was bewitched!

The huge knight laughed. The young woman rode up to Arthur. Smiling wickedly, she said, 'My mistress is Queen Morgan le Fay – your sister who wishes you nothing but ill!'

'Release me,' Arthur begged of the knight, 'and I will grant you any wish.'

'Very well,' replied the knight, 'but you must return in a year and a day and tell me what it is that women really want. Answer wrongly, and you die.'

Arthur then found himself free. His horse spun around and galloped out of control. When Arthur got back to his castle and told his story, his nephew Gawain promised to help him with his quest to find out what it was that women really wanted.

Arthur and Gawain asked everywhere. They collected whole books of answers. Yet a year later, they were still not sure. Sadly, they travelled towards the dark castle to meet the huge knight. Then, near the end of their journey, on a bare hillside, they met a lady dressed in the finest clothes and jewels. Well-dressed she was, but her looks were hideous. Arthur and Gawain had never before seen such an ugly woman – her face red and twisted, her eyes bulging.

'Speak to me nicely,' she warned them. 'Your life depends on it!'

Of course, they were polite and it was lucky that they were, because the lady made them an offer. She would tell them them the correct answer to the huge knight's question – if Arthur promised to marry her.

Gawain could not let his king marry such an ugly woman. 'Let me take your place,' he insisted. Arthur reluctantly agreed, and the woman took Gawain – her future husband – aside and told him the answer.

'What women really want,' she said, 'is to rule over men.'

When Arthur and Gawain arrived at the dark castle, the Knight of Tarn Wathelyne was furious that they had found the right answer. He knew that his mistress Morgan le Fay, Arthur's evil sister, would not be pleased.

In due course, Gawain married his ugly bride, whose name he now found to be Lady Ragnell. On his wedding night, she said to him, 'Come husband, kiss me, now that we are man and wife.' She was as ugly as ever, but he thought he saw sadness and suffering deep in her eyes. Trying to treat her kindly, he forced himself to kiss her – and then turned away tearfully.

A soft voice made him turn around in wonder. In place of the ugly old woman, stood the most beautiful young woman he had ever seen.

'Because you have treated me well, the wicked magic of Morgan le Fay is broken. She bewitched me. But the magic is not quite ended yet. I can be fair by day and foul by night, or the other way round. You must choose.'

This was an almost impossible choice for Gawain. 'If you are foul by day, you will have to bear the disgust of the knights and their ladies. If you are foul by night, you will have to bear my disgust – which I fear I shall be unable to overcome. You must make the choice yourself.'

Lady Raglan was overjoyed. 'Now, my lord, by giving me the choice, you have broken the magic completely. I will be fair by day and night, and the best wife you could hope for!'

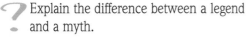

Try this

section round-up

? Explain the difference between a legend and a myth.

You should now know the difference between myths and legends, and understand how legends change as they are told.

? Imagine you are Gawain. Make a Mind Map to help you decide whether it is better for Lady Raglan to be fair by day or by night.

? Write the secret thoughts of Lady Raglan while Gawain tries to decide.

? What lessons do you think could be learnt from the story about how to behave?

? Retell the story to a friend, perhaps recording it. Then check to see what details you changed, added or missed out.

Take a break
before some heroics.

Heroes and dragons

How did English literature begin? With Stone Age hunting stories carved on cave walls? In fact, it began with poetry, spoken aloud by poets to an audience, probably helped by a musical instrument. The poets relied on memory, although some of the poems were very long. The poems were not even written down at first. Regular rhythms made them easier to memorise.

Most of these poems are **epics**. They tell stories about battles, great leaders, monsters and brave deeds. Below is part of the poem *Beowulf*, translated from Old English (Anglo-Saxon) into modern English. As you read it, remember that most listeners would have believed completely in the monster Grendel and in the strength and bravery of Beowulf.

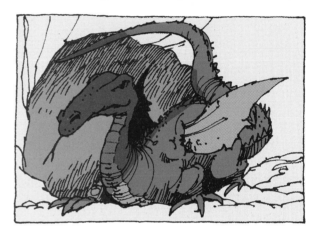

Beowulf and Grendel

Now Grendel, with the wrath of God on his back, came out of the moors and the mist-ridden fells with the intention of trapping some man in Heorot. Under the clouds he strode, until he came in sight of the rich banqueting hall glistening with plated gold. It was not the first time that he had paid a visit to Hrothgar's hall; but never before or afterwards did he experience such bad luck with its defenders. When the unhappy creature approached Heorot, the door, which was secured with wrought-iron bars, burst open at the touch of his talons. In his malicious fury he tore down the entrance of the building. Then the raging fiend, with horrible firelit eyes, stepped quickly upon the tessellated floor. Inside the hall he saw a great band of brothers-in-arms sleeping together, at which he laughed to himself, for the cruel demon, who meant to kill every single one of them before daybreak, saw before him the prospect of a huge feast.

But after that night it was not his luck to devour any more people. For Hygelac's mighty kinsman was watching to see how the marauder would set about his murderous business.

The fiend wasted no time, but for a start snatched up a sleeping man. He tore him apart in an instant, crunched the body, drank blood from its veins, and gulped it down in great bites until he had wholly swallowed the dead man, even the hands and feet. Then he advanced nearer. Reaching out with his open hand, the fiend was about to take hold of the hero on his bed. But Beowulf at once saw the hostile move and propped himself up on his elbow. The arch-beast soon realized that nowhere in the world had he ever met a man with such might in the grip of his hand. Although terror-struck, he could get away none the faster. He had never met anything like this in his life before; his one idea was to slink off to his hiding-place to rejoin the fellowship of devils. But at this point Beowulf remembered the promise which he had made earlier in the evening. He stood upright and gripped Grendel so tightly that the talons cracked to bursting. The monster fought to escape, but Beowulf closed with him. The fiend was trying to break loose and make a break for fen-refuge; yet, as he knew only too well, his talons were fast in an enemy clutch.

That was a fatal expedition which the demon made to Heorot. The hall thundered with the hubbub. Every one of the Danes who lived in the stronghold, soldiers and chieftains alike, was seized with extreme panic. The furious contestants for the mastery of the hall raged till the building rang. It was a miracle that the beautiful banqueting hall withstood such combatants without falling flat to the ground; but it was firmly braced inside and out with iron clamps forged by skilled craftsmen. They say that where the two antagonists fought, bench after bench inlaid with gold was uprooted from the floor.

Till then the most far-sighted among the Danes had never imagined that anybody might wreck their splendid ivory-inlaid hall by ordinary means, or destroy it by dint of cunning (barring fire, which would envelop it in flame). A stupendous din went up. Pure terror laid hold of the Danes, and of everyone outside the hall who heard the howling; the dreadful scream of God's adversary wailing his defeat the prisoner of hell bellowing over his wound. He was fast in the clutch of the strongest man alive.

THE ANGLO-SAXON CHRONICLE

A great fight took place today when the man-eating monster Grendel paid a visit to the hall of our leader Hrothgar. Grendel found the door wide open, and he had already eaten three men when Hygelac's relative Beowulf grabbed hold of him. The fight completely wrecked the hall, and Beowulf may now have to foot the bill for the damage.

Test yourself

? Correct the inaccuracies in the newspaper account above.

? Grendel is a 'raging fiend, with horrible firelit eyes'. What other phrases give a strong impression of him?

? Describe what details you would focus on if you were filming the scene. Design a poster advertising your film.

? With a partner, roleplay a reporter interviewing Beowulf, Grendel and a witness.

section round-up

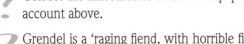

You have been looking at early English epic poetry and what it was about.

Don't try to be a hero: take a break!

The Bible and English literature

about this section
This section looks at the Bible's influence on English literature.

Myth or history?

Some people believe that all the events in the Bible actually happened. Others believe that some of these events – especially in the Old Testament – are **myths** (see start of chapter). This means that the events did not actually happen, even though they have an important meaning.

One example is the story of Adam and Eve in the garden of Eden, printed on this page. Many English writers have used this and other stories from the Bible.

The King James Bible

At one time the Bible was available only in Latin, and so only educated people could read it. Ordinary people had to trust the priests to tell them what it contained. Many people thought that translating it was a terrible sin. One translator, William Tyndale, was eventually burnt at the stake in 1536.

By the time James I became King of England in 1603, things had changed. He ordered a new translation of the Bible to be made by a committee of six men. It had to be in clear, simple English and sound good when read aloud. It had a big influence on the style of English writers.

Adam and Eve *(Genesis, Chapter 3)*

Now the serpent was more subtle than any beast of the field which the Lord God had made. And he said unto the woman, Yea, hath God said, Ye shall not eat of every tree of the garden?

And the woman said unto the serpent, We may eat of the fruit of the trees of the garden: But of the fruit of the tree which is in the midst of the garden, God hath said, Ye shall not eat of it, neither shall ye touch it, lest ye die.

And the serpent said unto the woman, Ye shall not surely die: For God doth know that in the day ye eat thereof, then your eyes shall be opened, and ye shall be as gods, knowing good and evil.

And when the woman saw that the tree was good for food, and that it was pleasant to the eyes, and a tree to be desired to make one wise, she took of the fruit thereof, and did eat, and gave also unto her husband with her; and he did eat.

John Milton

Milton was a great English poet. His long poem *Paradise Lost* (1667) tells the story of Adam and Eve. When Eve meets the serpent, she is amazed that he can speak:

> *Thee, serpent, subtlest beast of all the field*
> *I knew, but not with human voice endowed.*

He tells her that he can speak because he has eaten a special fruit and takes her to it. When they arrive, she tells him:

> *Of the fruit*
> *Of each tree in the garden we may eat,*
> *But of the fruit of this fair tree amidst*
> *The garden, God hath said, Ye shall not eat*
> *Thereof, nor shall ye touch it, lest ye die.*

Eve is persuaded in the end. Milton describes the awful moment when she reaches for the fruit, and eats:

> *Forth reaching to the fruit, she plucked,*
> *   she eat:*
> *Earth felt the wound, and Nature from*
> *   her seat*
> *Sighing through all her words gave signs*
> *   of woe,*
> *That was all lost.*

Practice time

 Read the extracts from the Bible, and from Milton, aloud. How do they sound?

 Copy or underline the words or phrases that are different from modern English. Write the modern English beside them.

 Compare the extracts. How has Milton been influenced by the Bible?

section round-up

This section has told you how about the importance of the Bible in English literature, and about the influence of the King James Version on writers such as Milton.

Geoffrey Chaucer

about this section

This section tells you about the early English poet Geoffrey Chaucer, and gives you an example from one of his *Canterbury Tales*.

Chaucer is probably the earliest English writer whose work you will ever read, except in translation. He was born in 1340 and died in 1400. During his life he was a servant to the King, a palace official, a Customs officer and a soldier – as well as a respected poet.

Chaucer is famous for his long poem called *The Canterbury Tales*. It is about a group of pilgrims travelling to Canterbury to show their dedication to God. They gather together at a London inn and the owner decides to go with them. He suggests that they should pass the time by telling stories. Whoever tells the best story will be wined and dined by the others.

One of the pilgrims is the Pardoner. He makes his living by preaching against greed and by granting people forgiveness for their sins. They pay him for this forgiveness and for being allowed to kiss his 'holy' relics: bits of bone or cloth supposed to have come from saints.

The Pardoner has bulging eyes, shoulder-length wax-yellow hair and a little cap which he thinks is more fashionable than a hood. His tale is about three sinful men who live for pleasure. They go in search of Death and meet an old man who tells them where to find Death. Instead they find gold there. Two of the men send the third into town to get them food and drink while they guard the gold. While he is gone, the others plan to murder him, so that they can have the gold to themselves. Now read part of the Pardoner's Tale, below. The notes in the margin will help you.

'Now,' quod the firste, 'thou woost wel we be tweye,
And two of us shull strenger be than oon.
Looke whan that he is set, that right anoon
Arys as though thou woldest with hym pleye,
And I shal ryve hym thurgh the sydes tweye,
Whil that thou strogelest with hym as in game,
And with thy daggere looke thou do the same;
And thanne shal al this gold departed be,
My deere freend, bitwixen me and thee.'

woost: know

set: sitting down

ryve: stab (like 'rivet')

departed: shared out
deere: prononced 'dee-re'

Meanwhile, the third man is in town buying poison with which to kill the other two!
✪ How do you think the story ends? (See next page.)

Chaucer check

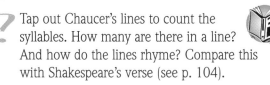

? Read the extract aloud. Try to sound like a would-be murderer!

? Tap out Chaucer's lines to count the syllables. How many are there in a line? And how do the lines rhyme? Compare this with Shakespeare's verse (see p. 104).

? Make notes or a Mind Map on what story you would tell if you were one of Chaucer's pilgrims.

section round-up

This section has introduced you to Geoffrey Chaucer and told you about one of his *Canterbury Tales*. How much can you remember about it?

4

SPELL-BINDING

To work some memory magic, remind yourself now of what you've learnt. If you've been making a chapter Mind Map, check it against the Mind Map on this page. Then try the checklist.

Answers

(p. 00): The Pardoner's Tale: The third man returns with the poison. The others kill him as planned. After this thirsty work they have a drink – and die because the third man has poisoned the bottle. The old man who told them where they could find Death was right after all!

checklist

Could you now:

	Yes	Not yet
1 Explain the difference between myths and legends? (pp. 33–5)	◯	◯
2 Say what a typical 'epic' poem is about? (p. 37)	◯	◯
3 Explain who Beowulf and Grendel are? (p. 37)	◯	◯
4 Say what was special about the King James Bible? (p. 39)	◯	◯
5 Explain why Chaucer's long poem is called *The Canterbury Tales*? (p. 41)	◯	◯

If your answer to any of these questions is 'Not yet', look back at the pages shown.
If you're still unsure, ask your teacher for help.

James I influence (Hermes) Mercury gods good evil.
history? BIBLE Milton beasts
myth? MYTHS about humans
changing stories LEGENDS stories oral changing
fact-based Arthur CHAUCER EPICS poems aloud memorised heroes Beowulf monsters Grendel Anglo-Saxons
language poet Tales Canterbury Pardoner
1340-1400

Fiction

overview

This chapter is about fiction. **Fiction** refers to writing that is made up rather than writing which gives facts. Works of fiction are works of the imagination. In your English course you will read **novels** and **stories** about fictional characters, and you will show your understanding and appreciation of them. This chapter will help you to:

- Know what to look for when you read fiction.

- Understand what is meant by style in fictional works.

- Appreciate writers' use of language.

- Discuss characters.

- Write about characters.

- Write about fiction written before 1900.

- Write about fiction written since 1900.

- Comment on the social context of literature.

- Recognise the way language in fiction has changed.

- Show understanding and appreciation of fiction from different cultures.

- Make comparisons.

This Mind Map shows you some of the things to think about when you are reading and writing about fiction. As you work through the chapter you may like to add your own ideas and examples to the Mind Map.

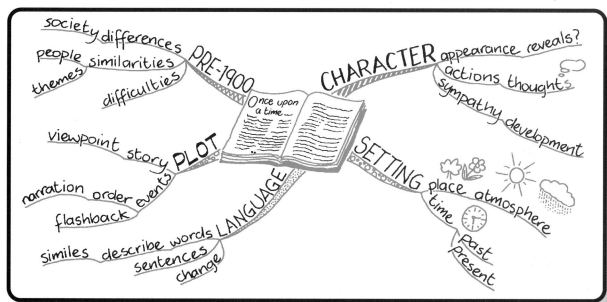

5

What to look for

about this section

This section will help you to identify and remember some of the main things to think about when you are reading a novel or a story.

Splat!

No, it's not the sound of a fly being swatted. It's a handy way of remembering some important words that you will need to use when you discuss and write about fiction.

S stands for **setting**. This is **where** and **when** the book is set. A story could be set in a school in the present day or in a school in the past or future. It could be set in another country or in an imaginary country.

P stands for **people** or **characters** – **who** the book is about. You will certainly be asked to discuss and write about the characters you meet in books. You might even be asked to pretend to be the characters.

L stands for the **language** in the book. When you discuss language you are discussing **style**. This is to do with **how** the book is written, the kinds of words and sentences the writer uses. There is more about this in the next section.

A stands for **action** or **plot**. This is **what** happens, the order of events.

T stands for **tone** or feeling. Think about the overall atmosphere of the book – is it upbeat and optimistic, is it serious, thought-provoking, frightening, amusing, disturbing?

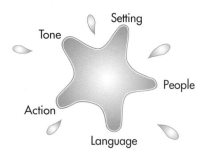

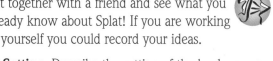

Try this

Get together with a friend and see what you already know about Splat! If you are working by yourself you could record your ideas.

Setting. Describe the setting of the book you are reading in class at the moment. What would be a good setting for: a murder mystery; a family coping with money difficulties; a group of aliens planning to take over another planet?

People or characters. Who is your favourite character in the book you are reading at the moment, or in a book you have read before? Who do you like the least? Remember to give your reasons. If you can, give examples from the book to support your points.

Language or style. You'll need a copy of your book for this. Find one expression that you think is very effective. It could be a description of someone or something, or a piece of dialogue. Read it to your friend.

Action or plot. Give a clear account of the plot of a book you know well.

Tone or feeling. Think of an episode in a book that made you feel sad. Tell your friend about it. Talk about parts of books that have made you feel angry or frightened.

section round-up

Now you should know some of the things to look for when you read fiction, and some of the words to use.

Take a break
before getting stylish.

Style

about this section

This section looks at how writers create particular effects through the way they write. It focuses on:

- Choice of words.
- Types of sentences.
- Points of view.
- Use of setting.

Winning words

Words are an important aspect of an author's style. Choosing just the right word to create a certain impression is a skill that takes a lot of hard work and practice. In the following sentences, the writer wants to make the reader aware of how tall the character is. ✪ Which sentence makes a stronger impression?

1 I saw that he was tall.
2 The first thing that struck me was his towering height.

Here, the word 'towering' suggests that the character rises above his surroundings as a tower rises to the sky. The word might also suggest something strong and imposing about the person.

WIZARD TIP

You will improve your grades in English if you comment on a writer's language. When you are answering a question about style, read the passage carefully and underline the words that you think are effective. Use phrases like 'This is effective because…'; 'This word/phrase/ expression gives me the impression that…'

Try this

Read this sentence and write a comment in the box about the writer's use of language.

Mr Wheeler thundered into the room and roared, 'Who broke the window?'

Stylish sentences

The style of a sentence can emphasise its meaning and add to the atmosphere the author wants to create. A writer can choose to write short, sharp sentences, or long, flowing ones. Good writing will usually show balance of sentence types, with writers selecting whichever type suits their purpose.

45

Do this

Read these short passages, then write words to describe each one in the boxes. Start with some words from the list.

1   The door creaked open. Luke froze. His hand closed around the knife in his pocket. It felt reassuring.

   ┌─────────────────────────────────┐
   │   │
   └─────────────────────────────────┘

2   The only movement was the gentle swaying of the hammock in the summer breeze and the slight quivering of the blades of grass, and the only sound to be heard was the rumble of a train in the distance.

   ┌─────────────────────────────────┐
   │   │
   └─────────────────────────────────┘

   tense   dreamy   hurried   dramatic   relaxed   peaceful .

Varying viewpoints

A story can be told from different points of view.

A writer can decide to use a **narrator**, sometimes called a **third-person** narrator, to tell the story.

Example: Elsie had lived all her life in the village. She knew every family, and knew all their secrets.

Another possibility is to use a **first-person** narrator. This is when one of the characters tells the story.

Example: I had lived all my life in the village. I knew every family, and knew all their secrets.

Try it out

Look at these examples of stories told from different points of view. With a friend, read the sentences out loud and discuss how well the choice of narrator fits in with what the sentence is saying (the content).

1   I felt the hairs on the back of my neck rise as I realised I wasn't alone in the room. I was sharing it with a body – a very dead body.

2   Marlon felt the hairs on the back of his neck rise as he realised he wasn't alone in the room. He was sharing it with a body– a very dead body.

3   Jessica and Lauren had been best friends from their very first day in junior school, but as they grew older the friendship became tinged with rivalry. When Jessica was chosen for the lead in the school play Lauren said she was delighted for her friend, but secretly she hoped that Jessica would turn out to be no good in the part.

4   Lauren has been my best friend ever since junior school. We've always quite enjoyed trying to beat each other in lessons and sport, but Lauren seemed genuinely delighted for me when I was given the lead part in the school play.

Each point of view has its advantages and disadvantages for the writer and the reader. Think of some of them. Add your ideas to the Mind Map.

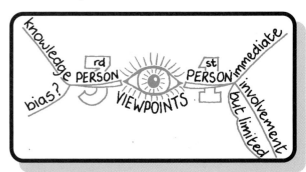

Super settings

The choice of **setting** and the way it is presented are important in fiction. The setting of a story – that is the place or places where it happens, the time in which it happens and features like the weather and the seasons – can be presented in different ways.

Your turn

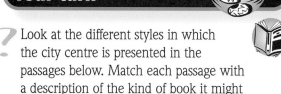

Look at the different styles in which the city centre is presented in the passages below. Match each passage with a description of the kind of book it might come from.

1 The horse's hoofs echoed on the cobbled streets and the cries of the street sellers could be heard as far as the town hall.
2 Dirty streets, harsh neon lights, empty burger cartons and scraps of newspaper wrapping themselves round your feet and legs – I was sick of this crummy town already.
3 The sun bathed the town hall in a golden glow that reflected Jan's feelings as she drove her brand new red sports car through the narrow city streets. As she rounded the curve at the bottom of the hill, a Land Rover coming in the opposite direction ...

A thriller **B** romance **C** historical novel

The answers are at the end of this chapter.

The picture shows some settings for novels or stories.
In what kind of style would you describe each one? Choose from the suggestions given below, and add your own.

- quite long sentences, to suggest relaxed atmosphere
- dialogue with lots of slang and colloquial expressions
- adjectives describing attractive colours
- short sentences, to create conflict and tension between characters
- adjectives suggesting a grey and grim atmosphere

If you would like some practice, choose one of the settings and write a description or a story.

section round-up

You should now be clued-up about some aspects of style, and should be able to comment on writers' use of language.

47

Character

about this section

This section will teach you what to look for in fictional characters and how to write about them.

How to discover what a character is like

Here are some ways to establish what kind of person the character is. Think about:

- what the character **looks** like
- what the character **does** and how he or she does it
- what the character **says** and how he or she says it
- what the character **thinks** and **feels**
- what **other characters** think of the character.

Sometimes you won't find an answer to all these questions. A writer may depict character in a few of these ways only, or perhaps through just one technique. It's quite likely that you will be able to apply all these questions to a full-length novel, and some of them to a short story or extract from a novel.

WIZARD TIP FOR DISCUSSING CHARACTER

Divide a sheet of paper into five columns, one for each of the headings above. Write the headings at the top of the columns. In each column, write down examples from the text. You could use a mixture of your own words and short quotations. Make one of these sheets for each of the main characters. If you are working on a novel or play, you may find it useful to use an A3 sheet or a sheet of sugar paper. If you prefer, you could write your notes on file paper, then cut them out and stick them on to a big sheet. A different colour for each character is helpful.

What the character looks like

Read this description of the appearance of a character called Mrs Tow-wouse. It is from a novel called *Joseph Andrews*, by Henry Fielding, published in 1742.

> Her person was short, thin, and crooked. The top of her nose was sharp and red and would have hung over her lips, had not Nature turned up the end of it. Her lips were two bits of skin, which, whenever she spoke, she drew together in a purse. Her chin was peaked; and at the upper end of that skin, which composed her cheek, stood two bones, that almost hid a pair of small red eyes.

Try this

? Underline all the **adjectives** (words that describe) you can find. What impression of the character do they create?

? Draw Mrs Tow-wouse's nose in the box provided.

? Read this sentence and cross out the words that you disagree with.
The description of Mrs Tow-wouse's appearance suggests that her character is

kind / harsh / warm / lovable / stern / mean / generous.

What the characters do and how they do it

The following extract is taken from *Walkabout*, a novel by James Vance Marshall. The book tells the story of two children, Mary and Peter, who are lost in the Australian desert. They meet a bush boy, a native Australian Aborigine, who helps them to survive. Here, the bush boy makes a fire.

> Peter followed the bush boy slavishly, copying his every move. Together, with sharp flints, they scooped a hollow out of the sandstone, about three feet square and nine inches deep. Then they started to forage for wood. They found it in plenty along the fringe of the desert. Yacca-yaccas: their tall, eight-foot poles, rising out of the middle of every tuffet of grass. The bush boy wrenched out the older poles; those that were dry, brittle with the saplessness of age. Then, among the roots, he fossicked [*searched about*] for resin. This resin was dry and wax-like, nature's ready-made firelighter.
>
> Following the bush boy's example, Peter snapped off the smaller poles, and hunted assiduously [*in a hardworking and persevering way*] for resin.

Your turn

? Look at the actions performed by Peter and by the bush boy. With a coloured pencil underline the words that describe Peter's actions. With a different colour, underline the words that describe the bush boy's actions. Finally, with a third colour, underline the words that describe what they do together.

? Tick the statements you agree with:

From the characters' actions in the extract, I can tell that:
- Peter knows what to do in the desert.
- Peter works with the bush boy.
- Peter doesn't think the bush boy can teach him anything.
- The bush boy doesn't know what wood to choose to make the fire.
- Peter learns from the bush boy.
- Peter is lazy.
- The bush boy is experienced at making fire.

5

What the characters say and how they say it

Here is an extract from *The Endless Steppe*, written by Esther Hautzig and published in 1968. The novel is a true account of how ten-year-old Esther and her family were sent to Siberia by the Russians in 1941. Here, Makrinin, the director of the mine in which they are working, gives out the tasks.

When he came to our family, Makrinin greeted my father with a courteous hello.

'I understand that you are an electrical engineer by profession. Here we have nothing like that for you to do. However ... we are in need of someone to drive a horse and cart.'

My father shrugged. 'I have ridden horses, but I have never driven one, nor harnessed one. I will do my best.'

'Yes, that is a good idea.' He turned to my mother. 'You ... you will work with a group of women and you will be in charge of them...'

'What kind of work?'

'Dynamiting the mines.'

'Dynamiting?' Mother's overheated face went white.

Father broke in. 'Oh please – why can't I do this? My wife could drive the buggy, that she could do I'm sure – '

Makrinin flushed. 'The orders are for the men to drive carts and work in the mine. The women will dynamite, the children will work in the fields, and the old people will shovel the gypsum [*the mineral found in the mine*].' He was embarrassed. 'Those are my orders,' he said softly. 'Now you may return to the school and rest if you wish.' He turned away from us and went to the next group as quickly as he could.

Over to you

From the way the characters speak in this passage, we can find out something about the kind of people they are.

❓ Underline all the words that Makrinin speaks, and the words that describe the way he says them. What do they tell you about Makrinin's character? Add to the ideas in the speech bubble.

I think he's quite gentle. He speaks softly and.....

❓ Draw circles around the words spoken by the father. What do they tell you about (a) his attitude to the task he's given (remember that he is an electrical engineer by profession) (b) his feelings for his wife?

❓ Esther's mother says only five words in this passage, but they tell us something about her personality. Choose the words that could apply to her:

confident   nervous   panicky   bossy   unsure
shy   alarmed

What the characters think and feel

Writers often reveal characters' thoughts and feelings, giving us further insights into the lives and personalities of the people they are describing. In this extract from Gary Paulsen's novel *The Car*, published in 1994, we find out about 14-year-old Terry. One evening he realises that his parents are not coming home.

He was alone.

His name was Terry Anders. He was fourteen years old, living in Cleveland, Ohio, and his parents had left him.

Of course it didn't happen quite that suddenly. The first call came at almost exactly eight o'clock. His mother called first.

'Terry, I'm not coming home. I can't take it any longer. I've taken all my things. Tell your father I won't be there to fight him any longer. You'll both have to do without me.' And she hung up.

He had said almost nothing. Had once more felt a sense of wonder – this time at why he didn't seem to care all that much that his mother had gone. A part of him felt bad, but it was mostly because he *didn't* feel bad that he felt bad. She was gone – that thought was there – and there wouldn't be any more fights.

His father called just after nine.

'Tell your mother I'm not coming back – I've got all my stuff. I'm sick of the whole thing.' And he hung up.

Terry put the phone back and looked out the window at the road in the darkness and thought: *So, they aren't going to be here. Neither one. At least for a little while. Mother thinks I'm staying here with Father and Father thinks I'm staying here with Mother.*

I'm alone.

Just me.

And the house.

Oh yes, he thought, *and a smile came, widened into a grin. There's one other thing.*

The car.

WIZARD TIP

Often a writer will use a word like 'felt' or 'thought' when describing a characters' reactions. This makes it quite easy for you to understand a character's thoughts and feelings. Watch out for places where thoughts and feelings are **suggested** or **implied**.

Now try this

? Find the places in the passage where the words 'thought' or 'felt' are used. What do Terry's thoughts and feelings tell you about him? A Mind Map has been started for you. Add your ideas to it.

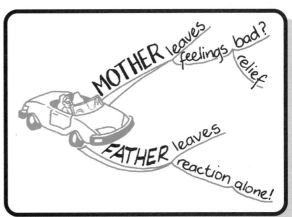

? Terry's feelings about his parents' fights are suggested. What are they?

? The writer lets us know how Terry feels when he realises he's alone. What device does the author use to show how Terry gradually takes in the situation? (Look at the way the words are arranged on the page.)

? What do you think Terry thinks and feels when he realises that the car has been left?

? You could write the rest of the story. What might happen to Terry – and the car? Make a Mind Map to plan your ideas.

What other characters think of him

Another way of discovering what a character  is like is by looking at how other people react to him or her. In this extract from *Great Expectations* by Charles Dickens, published in 1861, we see some aspects of the character of Mr Jaggers, a criminal lawyer, through what his clients think of him.

There were two men of secret appearance lounging in Bartholomew Close, one of whom said to the other when they first passed me that 'Jaggers would do it if it was to be done.' There was a knot of three men and two women standing at a corner, and one of the women was crying on her dirty shawl, and the other comforted her by saying, as she pulled her own shawl over her shoulders, 'Jaggers is for him, Amelia, and what more *could* you have?'

At length, I saw Mr Jaggers coming across the road towards me. All the others who were waiting saw him at the same time, and there was quite a rush at him. He addressed himself to his followers. First, he took the two secret men.

'Now, I have nothing to say to you,' said Mr Jaggers. 'I want to know no more than I know. As to the result, it's a toss-up. Have you paid Wemmick?' [*His clerk*]

'We made the money up this morning, sir,' said one of the men, submissively, while the other perused [*examined carefully*] Mr Jaggers's face.

'I don't ask when you made it up, or where, or whether you made it up at all. Has Wemmick got it?'

'Yes, sir,' said both men together.

Over to you

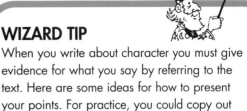

? What do Mr Jaggers's clients say about him? What does this tell you about how successful a lawyer he is?

? What do you gather from the way his clients wait for him, then rush towards him?

? How do the men speak to Mr Jaggers? What does this tell you about Jaggers's character?

? You can find out more about Mr Jaggers from this passage by looking at what he says and how he speaks to his clients. Why do you think Mr Jaggers wants to know as little as possible about their crimes? What *is* he very concerned to know?

? Write a paragraph about Mr Jaggers's character. Use quotations and references from the passage to illustrate your points.

? Choose a character from a book you know well. Prepare a short talk about the character. Use the book for short references to illustrate your points, or copy them out. If you like, ask your teacher if you can give the talk to your group or class.

WIZARD TIP

When you write about character you must give evidence for what you say by referring to the text. Here are some ideas for how to present your points. For practice, you could copy out these sentences and fill in the gaps with references from one of your texts.

I think that (character's name) is .... and .... For example, she .....

An incident that illustrates (character's name)'s .... is where he ....

section round-up

Well done! You've learnt about what to look for in fictional characters, and have practised some techniques to help you to understand and write about the characters you meet in books.

Have a break before delving into the past.

Comparing pre-1900 and modern fiction

Happiest days

It has been said that schooldays are the happiest days of your life. You may agree or disagree with this statement – although you probably won't be able to make a judgement until your schooldays are well behind you. Many modern writers and writers in earlier centuries have described school experiences. This may be because a school setting gives scope to explore aspects of fiction such as character. Think about the different people and personalities you find in schools! The Mind Map shows some ideas about what you might find developed in stories and novels about school life. You could copy it and add your own thoughts.

This extract is from *David Copperfield* by Charles Dickens, published in 1869.

School began in earnest, next day. A profound impression was made upon me, I remember, by the roar of voices in the schoolroom suddenly becoming hushed as death when Mr Creakle entered after breakfast, and stood in the doorway looking round upon us like a giant in a storybook surveying his captives.

Here I sit at the desk watching his eye as he rules a ciphering book for another victim whose hands have just been flattened by the ruler, and who is trying to wipe the sting out with a pocket handkerchief. I don't watch his eye in idleness, but because I am morbidly attracted to it in a dread desire to know what he will do next, and whether it will be my turn to suffer or someone else's.

A lane of small boys beyond me, with the same interest in his eye, watch it too. I think he knows it, though he pretends he doesn't. An unhappy culprit, found guilty of imperfect exercise, approaches at his command. The culprit falters excuses and professes a determination to do better tomorrow. Mr Creakle cuts a joke before he beats him, and we laugh at it – miserable little dogs, we laugh with our visages as white as ashes, and our hearts sinking into our boots.

Comprehension

Some of the expressions in the passage may be unfamiliar to you. However, you can often work out what an unfamiliar expression means from your understanding of what's going on in the passage. This exercise should show you that it's not difficult to get the general sense of a piece of writing.

Circle what you think is the most likely meaning of the words in italics:

1   watching his eye as *he rules a cipher book* for another victim whose hands ...

(a) This means that Mr Creakle writes down rules in a book.

(b) This means that Mr Creakle writes in code.

(c) This means that Mr Creakle draws lines in an exercise book.

2   An unhappy culprit, *found guilty of imperfect exercise*, approaches ...

(a) This means that the pupil hadn't done the compulsory PE exercises.

(b) This means that the pupil had made mistakes in his schoolwork.

(c) This means that the pupil had done only some of the required PE exercises.

3   The culprit *professes a determination to do better tomorrow.*

(a) This means that the pupil is determined to find a better profession.

(b) This means that the pupil says that he will be more determined tomorrow.

(c) This means that the pupil says that he will do better tomorrow.

You can check your answers at the end of this chapter.

Which of these words could you use in a description of the relationship between the boys and Mr Creakle? Underline the words you choose.

respect   awe   fear   liking   tension   security
friendship   light-heartedness   nervousness
cruelty   pain   apprehension

Find two similes in the first paragraph. (Remember: a **simile** is a comparison that uses the words 'like' or 'as'.) What impression of Mr Creakle do they create?

The word 'profess' indicates speaking, or declaring. There are lots of words you can use instead of 'say' or 'said'. Add to this list:

shout
whisper
complain
insist

This extract is from *Jane Eyre*, by Charlotte Brontë, published in 1847.

During January, February and part of March, the deep snows, and after their melting, the almost impassable roads, prevented our stirring beyond the garden walls, except to go to church, but within these limits we had to pass an hour every day in the open air. Our clothing was insufficient to protect us from the severe cold; we had no boots, the snow got in our shoes, and melted there; our ungloved hands became numbed and covered with chilblains, as were our feet. I remember the torture of thrusting the swelled, raw and stiff toes into my shoes in the morning. Then the scanty supply of food was distressing. From the deficiency of nourishment resulted an abuse which pressed hardly on the younger pupils: whenever the famished great girls had an opportunity they would coax or menace the little ones out of their portion. Many a time I have shared between two claimants the precious morsel of brown bread distributed at teatime, and after relinquishing to a third half the contents of my mug of coffee, I have swallowed the remainder with an accompaniment of secret tears, forced from me by the exigency of hunger.

[*Mr Brocklehurst, the school governor, punishes Jane when she drops her slate.*]

'A careless girl!' said Mr Brocklehurst. 'Let the girl who broke her slate come forward!'

Of my own accord, I could not have stirrred, but two girls who sat on each side of me pushed me towards the dread judge.

'Fetch that stool,' said Mr Brocklehurst, pointing to a very high one. 'Place the child upon it.'

And I was placed there, by whom I don't know. They hoisted me up to the height of Mr Brocklehurst's nose.

Said he, 'Teachers and children, you all see this girl?'

Of course they did; for I felt their eyes directed like burning-glasses against my scorched skin.

Comprehension

What hardships does Jane Eyre describe?

Underline the words that emphasise the physical pain the pupils experienced.

What were Jane's feelings when she was singled out by Mr Brocklehurst?

'an abuse which pressed hardly on the younger pupils' – re-write this expression in a more modern form.

This extract is from *Flour Babies* by Anne Fine, published in 1992.

Mr Cartwright swung his legs to and fro under the desk, and raised his voice over the waves of bad-tempered muttering.

'Don't worry if you feel you can't give this your full attention now, 4C,' he said to his new class. 'I'll be delighted to go over it again in your break-time.'

Some of them visibly made a bit of an effort. A few pens were pulled out of a few mouths. One or two of the boys swivelled their heads back from the riveting sight of the janitor painting large white numbers on the dustbins. But, on the whole, the improvement was pitiful. Half of them looked as if they'd left their brains at home. The other half looked as if they didn't have any.

'Buck up,' he told them. 'This shouldn't take all day. I'll run through the choices one last time, and then you'll have to vote. Now pay attention, everyone.'

Shifting his vast bottom round, he tapped the blackboard on which, five minutes earlier, he'd chalked up the options for 4C's contribution to the school Science Fair,

> textiles
> nutrition
> domestic economy
> child development
> consumer studies

reciting them aloud again, for those who had trouble with reading.

A swell of grumbling rose over the fidgets and whispers and shuffling feet, and the creak of chairs being tipped back dangerously on two of their four legs.

'It isn't fair, sir.'

'Boring!'

'You can't call that lot Science. It's not right.'

What's going on?

How does the class behave? Underline words in the extract that describe their behaviour.

What does Mr Cartwright think of his class? Draw a circle around the words in the extract that tell you this.

What task does the class have to do?

How does the class respond to the choices they've been given?

Task time

Look at language

? The language used in *Flour Babies* is more colloquial than the language of the other two extracts. Find two colloquial expressions. (**Colloquial** refers to the kind of everyday language we use when we speak to each other. Look at the Wizard Wordbox in Chapter 6.)

? Decide which book, **1** *David Copperfield*, **2** *Jane Eyre* or **3** *Flour Babies*, each of these quotations comes from. (Answers at the end of this chapter.)

A 'There is a strange unwholesome smell upon the schoolroom, like mildewed corduroys, sweet apples wanting air, and rotten books.'

B 'I know most of you have the boredom thresholds of brain-damaged gnats.'

C 'I toiled hard, and my success was proportionate to my efforts; my memory improved with practice; exercise sharpened my wits.'

Look at sentences

? Which extract has the shortest sentences?

? Look at the second sentence of the *Jane Eyre* extract. What punctuation mark does the writer use to break up parts of the sentence? Write it here:

WIZARD TIP

The punctuation mark above is called a **semi-colon**. You will help to raise your grade if you show that you can use it properly. A **semi-colon** shows a pause that is longer than a comma. It can be used to join two complete sentences together to make one sentence – but only if the two sentences are closely connected. It is often used to create a sense of contrast and balance.

Example: She held the cup in both hands; the warmth of the drink comforted her.

Headingley is a cricket ground; Old Trafford is a football stadium.

Look at subject matter

? What do the three extracts have in common?

? What differences do the extracts show about school life in the nineteenth century and in the modern day? The Mind Map shows some ideas. You could add your own examples from the passages.

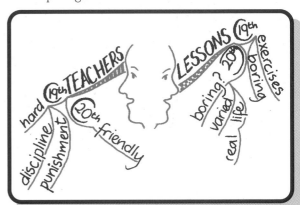

? Imagine that you are one of the pupils in the school in *Jane Eyre*. Write a letter home describing your experiences.

? Write an account of a day in your life at school. Try to include description and conversation.

? Explain to a friend who is about to read a novel by Charles Dickens or Charlotte Brontë some of the differences between fiction of their period and modern fiction.

section round-up

If you've worked your way through this section you have read extracts from nineteenth-century and twentieth-century novels and can discuss their differences and similarities.

Take a break before going on.

Comparing fiction from different cultures

about this section

This section concentrates on writers who come from a different background and culture from those within the English literary tradition. When we refer to 'the English literary tradition' we mean the kind of writer you meet in this book: William Shakespeare, Henry Fielding, Charles Dickens, Charlotte Brontë, Laurie Lee. When we refer to 'culture' we mean the shared ideas and lifestyles of a particular social or ethnic group.

So writers from a different culture will include poets, novelists and dramatists from countries like Africa, America, Australia, India.

As you work through this section you will:

● Read fiction from different cultures.

● Appreciate aspects of life in different cultures.

● Make relevant comparisons.

Pumpkin-heads

This extract is adapted from *The Village by the Sea* by Anita Desai. The novel tells the story of a poor family in Thul, a fishing village on the western coast of India. Hari, the 14-year-old boy, finds out about plans to build an industrial complex in the village.

'No, but tell me,' Hari said eagerly. 'What will they make at the factory?'

'Fertiliser, I told you.' The man sounded impatient.

'What is that?' Hari asked.

The man had to smile, however grimly. These villagers were such pumpkin-heads, they knew nothing. 'Chemicals,' he said, using another word that Hari did not know. 'Different kinds of chemicals to put in the ground – nitrogen, ammonia, urea – to make things grow.'

'Oh, *manure*?' asked Hari, deeply disappointed. All this vast complex, modern and scientific, to be built only to make manure for the fields?

'No, not manure, pumpkin-head. This is to stop people from following their cows and buffaloes around and collecting their dung to put in their miserable fields. Here the factories will produce tons and tons of chemicals to be sent all over the country and sold to farmers. Rich farmers,' he added, with another scornful look at Hari's torn shirt and bare feet. 'They will need people to work. People from all over India will get jobs here.'

'And what about us?' Hari cried, running after him. 'I need a job.'

Suddenly the man stopped glaring. His face softened and his eyes looked kinder. 'So,' he said, 'you need a job, eh? Hungry, eh? No food in the house? Sick mother, drunken father, sisters to be married off and no dowries, eh?'

Hari was so astonished that he gave a gasp. How did this stranger know about his family? Had he been finding out about him?

The man spun round with the same expression of scorn cutting across his face. 'You villagers – you're all the same. Pumpkin-heads. Drink toddy and lie drunk under the coconut trees all day. Go fishing and drown yourself in the sea. Leave the women to manage. Old women and girls going hungry in the village. What a place, your Thul. What a bunch of pumpkin-heads.'

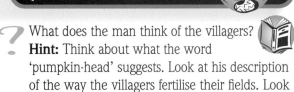

Question time

? What does the man think of the villagers?
Hint: Think about what the word 'pumpkin-head' suggests. Look at his description of the way the villagers fertilise their fields. Look at his description of their way of life.

? What does the man think of Hari?
Hint: How does he look at Hari's appearance? Underline the phrase that describes this. Find the place where his expression changes. What might he be thinking at this point? Why does he become scornful again?

? What impression of Hari do you receive?
Hint: Think about what his appearance tells you. Which two words doesn't he understand? What does this tell you? What do you learn about his family and their way of life?

Frankie Mae

Frankie Mae is the title of a story by Jean Wheeler Smith, an Afro-American writer, which describes the harsh childhood of a black girl growing up in Mississippi in the 1930s.

The Old Man [Frankie Mae's father] and his wife, Mattie, worked hard that year. Up at four-thirty and out to the field. Frankie Mae stayed behind to nurse the other children and to watch the pot that was cooking for dinner. At sundown, they came back home and got ready for the next day. They did a little sweeping, snapped some beans for dinner the next day. Then they sat on the porch together for maybe a half hour.

That was the time the Old Man liked best, the half hour before bed. He and Frankie talked about what had happened during the day, and he assured her that she had done a good job keeping up the house. Then he went on about how smart she was going to be when she started school. It would be in two years, when the oldest boy was big enough to take care of the others.

One evening on the porch Frankie said, 'A man from town came by today looking for our stove. Said we was three weeks behind and he was gonna take it.'

The Old Man lowered his head. He was ashamed that Frankie had had to face that man by herself. He'd have to start teaching her how to deal with folks like that.

'What did you tell him, baby?' he asked. 'He didn't hurt you none, did he?'

'No, he didn't bother me, sides looking mean. I told him I just this morning seen some money come in the mail from Uncle Ed in Chicago. And I heard my daddy say he was gonna use it to pay off the stove man. So he said, "Well, I give y'all one more week, one more." And he left.'

The Old Man pulled Frankie to him and hugged her. 'You did 'zactly right, honey.' She understood. She would be able to take care of herself.

Over to you

What do you learn about Frankie's way of life?
Hint: Underline the tasks she has to do. Find the lines that tell you how old she is! How do you know that the family was poor?

What do you learn about the relationship between Frankie and her father?
Hint: Look at the description of them sitting on the porch together. Look at the Old Man's reaction when he hears about the stove man's visit.

What do you find out about Frankie's character?
Hint: Think about the way Frankie deals with the stove man. Look at what her father thinks about the way she handled it.

What do you notice about the language the characters use? Copy out two examples of **dialect** and re-write them in standard English. (Look back at Chapter 1 for a reminder about **dialect**.)

Comparing passages

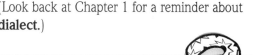

What do you find similar and different about the characters and their situations? Explore your ideas in a Mind Map. One has been started here for you.

section round-up

You have shown understanding and appreciation of writing from different cultures, and have practised techniques for looking closely at the text.

5

SPELL-BINDING

To work some memory magic, remind yourself
of what you've learnt. If you've been adding
to a chapter Mind Map, review it now.
Then try the checklist.

checklist

Could you now:

	Yes	Not yet
1 Know what to look for when you read fiction? (p. 44)	◯	◯
2 Write about characters in fiction? (pp. 48–53)	◯	◯
3 Feel confident about reading pre-1900 fiction? (pp. 54–8)	◯	◯
4 Feel confident about reading modern fiction? (pp. 54–8)	◯	◯
5 Discuss differences in language? (p. 58)	◯	◯
6 Feel confident about reading fiction from different cultures? (pp. 59–61)	◯	◯

If your answer to any of these questions is 'Not yet', look back at the pages shown. If you are still unsure,
ask your teacher for help.

Non-fiction

overview

Types of non-fiction

about this section

What is meant by non-fiction?

Non-fiction is the expression we use when we refer to writing that gives information. The information may be facts, opinions, instructions, stories of people's travels or their lives. Unlike fiction, non-fiction writing consists of factual accounts and isn't based on imaginative or made-up stories. However, good non-fiction writing requires the same range of skills as good fiction writing:

- careful and sensitive choice of words
- accuracy in grammar, spelling and punctuation
- awareness of purpose and audience.

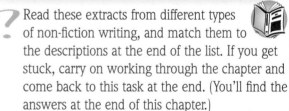

Try this

Read these extracts from different types of non-fiction writing, and match them to the descriptions at the end of the list. If you get stuck, carry on working through the chapter and come back to this task at the end. (You'll find the answers at the end of this chapter.)

1 Up early. At noon came my good guests. I had a pretty dinner for them – six roasted chickens, and salmon hot, for the first course.
2 Foxes have become a nuisance in some urban areas, threatening the safety of domestic animals and tearing open dustbin bags.
3 Support the Bill – stop hunting now!
4 My legs gave way beneath me and I felt a searing pain in my ankle.
5 Within two hours a short flight will bring you to this magnificent city with its spellbinding scenery and picturesque ports.
6 This was an exciting performance, finally demonstrating that Mirage are likely to last the course and prove more substantial than their name.
7 This injury was one which was to affect the rest of his sporting career.
8 I lay awake in the hotel room. Impressions of the city swam in front of my eyes.

9 Finally persuaded them to let me go to Mirage at Wembley Arena! Now I've just got to find the money!

10 At five o'clock I was off ahead and came to a field which I had been told I should meet with. I cast about in my mind as to what method would be best to employ in crossing this expanse of mud.

A Autobiography
B Travel brochure
C Diary written before this century.
D Informative article about urban wildlife.
E Travel account written before this century.
F Biography
G Review
H Diary entry
I Travel account
J Leaflet
K Magazine article

Number	Letter
1	
2	
3	
4	
5	
6	
7	
8	
9	
10	

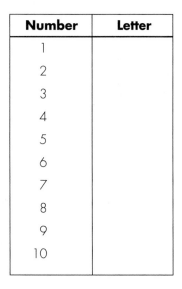

Reading non-fiction

The variety of non-fiction may seem a little overwhelming. You might feel that you don't know what to look for, or where to start. Don't worry – it's not half as difficult as you think. There are a few key questions that will keep you on the right track, whether you are reading an informative article, a guide book, a biography or any other types of non-fiction writing.

- What is the **purpose** of the writing? Is it intended to persuade, to inform, to entertain? (Remember that a piece of writing may have more than one purpose.)
- Who is the intended **audience**? Who is going to read it?
- What is the **form**? Is it an article, a leaflet, an account, a poster, a brochure? What kind of language does it use?

WIZARD TIP

Apply the **PAF** technique when you read non-fiction.

Purpose

Audience

Form

When you have decided what is the purpose of the writing, who it is addressing and what form (e.g. letter, article, diagram, etc.) the writer has chosen, you can go on to think about how effective it is.

Task time

? Test your knowledge of **PAF**! Discuss with a friend (or your teacher if you like) what differences you would expect to find between:

(a) An Introduction to Science for primary school pupils and a Key Stage 3 Science textbook

(b) A leaflet about food hygiene to be distributed in supermarkets and a booklet of regulations for cafés and restaurants.

? Here is a Mind Map of types of non-fiction and what to be aware of when you read and write it. Add to the branches as you work through the chapter.

section round-up R

By now you should be familiar with:
• **Types of non-fiction.**
• **Important aspects of reading and writing non-fiction.**

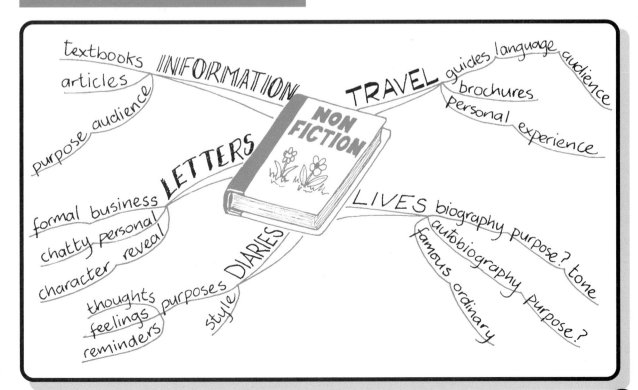

6

Letters

about this section

In this section you will focus on:

- **The reasons for writing letters.**

- **What letters can reveal about the people who write them.**

- **The differences between personal and formal letters.**

When did you last write a letter? It's possible that you have written only a few letters in your life – but this will probably change. You may need to write letters for all kinds of personal and business reasons, and you will be expected to follow the accepted rules of language and layout. You never know, your letters might be so interesting and reveal so much about your life and the world in which you live that they will be published for the information and enjoyment of others!

The Mind Map shows some of the reasons for writing a letter. Copy the Mind Map and add your own examples.

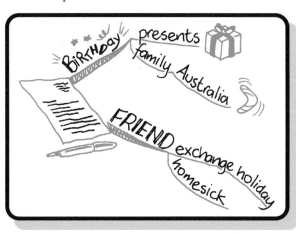

Made-up letters

Some books are made up entirely of letters! In books like this, the writers reveal character and plot through the letters that people write to each other.

Here are two letters from a novel called *French Leave* by Eileen Fairweather. The story is about a teenage girl called Maxine Harrison. See if you can discover what Maxine is like, and what she's up to!

> Dear Jean,
>
> Your postal order and present were the only things that stopped me from bursting into tears this morning. I'd said I wanted money for my birthday but Mum still went ahead and bought me her usual tasteless rubbish. God, she must think I'm twelve, getting me a Care Bears nightdress case and a 100 per cent pure gilt charm bracelet.
>
> Thank you for your interesting present, 'Cooking in a Bedsit'. I had a few anxious moments when I opened the parcel. Mum gave me one of her piercing 'what's-going-on' stares when I saw the title and hid it. I tried to act natural, even though I'd stuffed it up my shirt.
>
> Much love,
>
> Max

What's going on? ✪ What impression do you gain of Maxine's character? ✪ Why does Maxine hide the book from her mother? ✪ What could Maxine be planning? ✪ What are Maxine's feelings about her mother?

Dear Jean,

I'm here! I figured you'd be anxious to know if my getaway was a success. It was, though it did get a bit tricky at times. It's hard to act casual when your mum keeps giving you the 'I know something's up' eyeball. But I didn't crack under the pressure and am now relaxing happily in my own flat.

I have to confess, it was pretty sad packing up my stuff this morning while Dad was at his 900th job interview. I nearly cried in my room over my photos of Mum and Dad holding me when I was a baby. But they don't love me any more. For good measure, I pinned my goodbye note to the Care Bears.

Getting settled on my own was a bit daunting at first. But since I've cleaned the flat I feel much better. I got rid of the green furry thing rotting in the saucepan and I've sprayed all over with deodorant. Now the whole place whiffs of lily-of-the-valley, mixed with just a tinge of old sock. (Not mine.) I'd sleep with my window open but I'm on the ground floor.

I wish I'd brought the remains of Mum's cake. She went to a lot of effort really, writing 'Sweet Sixteen' in Smarties. I'd nip out for some more Pot Noodles from the late-night supermarket on the corner. But I'm a bit scared to go out here after dark on my own.

It's really fun.

Write soon. Please.

Max

What's going on? ✪ What has Maxine done? ✪ What was the flat like when she moved in? ✪ Find two details which show that Maxine is concerned about her safety. ✪ What are Maxine's feelings about her parents? ✪ What are Maxine's feelings about the flat and her situation?

Task time

Tick the statements you agree with.

- Maxine told her mother that she was moving into a flat. ☐
- Maxine left home without telling her parents. ☐
- Maxine's mother doesn't realise how grown-up Maxine is. ☐
- Maxine thinks her parents don't love her. ☐
- Maxine appreciates her mother's efforts for her birthday. ☐
- Maxine settled into her flat straight away. ☐
- Maxine is delighted to be in her flat, away from her parents. ☐
- Maxine has mixed feelings about her situation. ☐

Circle the words that you think describe Maxine.

helpless   organised   clever   uncertain   confident   cheerful   miserable   independent   cruel   determined

Choose a character from a book you have read. Think of an important event concerning that person. Write a letter about the event to another character in the book.

WIZARD TIP

You will sometimes be asked to write a letter from a character in a book. When you do this kind of task, remember to make your letter show **what the character is like** and **what is happening or has happened** in the book.

6

Firm words

Read these extracts from letters, one written by Florence Nightingale during the Crimean War, and the other by Charles Dickens to his sixth son, Henry.

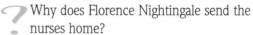

Over to you

? Why does Florence Nightingale send the nurses home?

? What does she feel about having to do this?

? What impression of her character do you gain from the letter?

? Ring the words that describe Charles Dickens's character and attitudes as seen in the letter.

generous   mean   extravagant
impatient with his son   concerned for his son
anxious about debt   not caring about debt
understanding of his son's needs   intolerant
lazy   hardworking   kind

Barrack Hospital Scutari
16 April 1885

I am sorry to be obliged to tell you that Thompson and Anderson, two of the nurses from Edinburgh, went out drinking on Saturday night. Anderson was brought back dead drunk. But Thompson I believe to be the most hardened offender. This was such a catastrophe that there was nothing to be done but to pack them off to England directly. It is a great disappointment, as they were hard-working good-natured women. Only one week's wages was due to them, which I have not given them, of course, as by rights they ought not to have a free passage home. There were no extenuating circumstances.

Ever your FN

15 October 1868

My dear Harry

I enclose you another cheque for twenty-five pounds, and I write to London by this post, ordering three dozen sherry, two dozen port, six bottles of brandy, and three dozen light claret, to be sent down to you.

Now, observe attentively. We must have no shadow of debt. Square up everything whatsoever that it has been necessary to buy. It appears to me that an allowance of two hundred and fifty pounds a year will be handsome for all your wants, if I send your wines.

You know how hard I work for what I get, and I think you know that I never had money help from any human creature after I was a child.

Whatever you do, above all other things keep out of debt and confide in me. If ever you find yourself on the verge of difficulty, come to me. You will never find me hard with you while you are manly and truthful.

Your affectionate father.

Different types of letter

Whether you are writing a personal letter or a formal letter, there are certain rules you should follow. A personal letter is one you would write to a friend or relative, or someone you know. This kind of letter is to do with your personal and family life. A formal letter is to do with business matters, and is the kind you would write to a company or organisation. Look at the different ways in which each type of letter is set out.

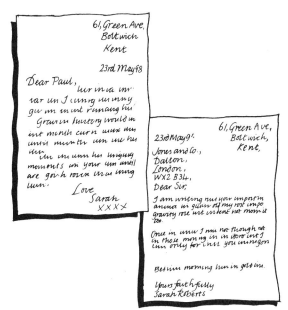

Try this

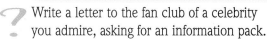

Write a letter to the fan club of a celebrity you admire, asking for an information pack.

Write a short letter to a friend who has moved away from your area. (The 'Wizard tip' will help you.)

WIZARD TIP

Remember to apply the **PAF** technique that you met at the beginning of this chapter. What is the **purpose** of your letter? (It might be to keep your friend informed about what's been going on; to make arrangements for a meeting during the hoidays, etc). Remember the **audience** and **form**. You are writing to a friend, so a casual informal style will be appropriate. However, there is also a secondary **audience** – your teacher or an examiner. Use your judgement!

WIZARD WORDBOX

One of the ways to improve your grade is to show that you understand the difference between formal language and informal language. Look at the letters from Maxine at the beginning of this section. Here are some of the informal expressions she uses. Write beside each one a more formal version.

eyeball   whiffs   nip

section round-up

You've learnt about different kinds of letters, and what letters tell us about their writers' characters and lives. Well done!

Now take a break – make a note in your diary!

6

Diaries

about this section

In this section you will look at:

- Reasons for writing diaries.

- Diaries written recently, and in the nineteenth century.

- The use of language in diary writing.

- What we can learn from reading diaries.

You may have kept a diary at some point in your life, if only for a few days. Probably you recorded what you did that day, or jotted down a reminder of things you had to do. Some diaries are private and intended for personal use only, others are written with a more public audience in mind. The Mind Map shows some of the reasons for writing diaries. Copy it and add your own ideas.

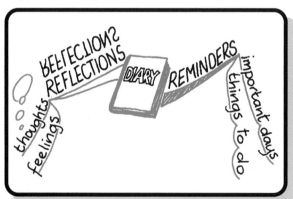

Whose diary?

1
Lousy day! C. still not speaking to me.
Cried myself to sleep.

2
Remember to pick up Jamie's birthday present.

Pay electricity bill!

7.30. Parents/teachers meeting.

3
Went to cinema with Jules and Darren. Funny, I don't like being with them as much as I used to.

4
Princess Diana died early this morning. Everyone's shocked and sad.

5
Christmas Day in Australia — strange to be spending it on the beach!

Task time

? What kind of person might have written each of these diary extracts?

? Are some extracts more private than others?

? What do you notice about the language in some of the entries? For example, are they all written in full sentences?

Zlata and Sarah

Zlata, a young Yugoslavian girl, wrote her
diary in the 1990s during the war in Sarajevo.
She called her diary Mimmy.

Wednesday 29 July 1992

Dear Mimmy
Mummy came home from work in tears
today. She had very, very sad news.
Mladjo was killed in front of his house
yesterday. The funeral was today, she
read it in the papers, but it was too
late. Awful. What's happening here is
unbelievable. People are getting
killed, disappearing, being buried, and
their closest friends can't even
attend the funeral. His family don't
even know that he's dead. And who
knows when they'll hear the sad news,
because Sarajevo is cut off from the
rest of the world. The phones aren't
working. God, what is happening?

Tuesday 26 January 1993

Dear Mimmy
I'm getting ready to go to Nejra's
birthday party. I'm wearing black
tights (thick of course), a red
turtleneck under a white blouse,
a kilt and red cardigan sweater.
As you can see, I've dressed up.
Mimmy, I've noticed that I don't
write to you any more about the
war or the shooting. That's
probably because I've become used
to it. All I care about is that the
shells don't fall within 50 metres
of my house, that we've got wood,
water, and of course, electricity. I
can't believe I've become used to
all this, but it seems I have.
Whether it's being used to it,
fighting for survival or something
else, I don't know.

Monday 1 February 1993

Dear Mimmy
It's February. In three days it will
have been ten months of hell, blood,
horror. Today is Kenan's birthday. We
can't go, because they're shooting
again. God, I keep thinking this is
going to stop, but the war just goes
on and on.

Think about this. ✪ What impression do you
gain of Zlata's character? ✪ What does her
diary tell you about what living through a war
is like?

71

The extracts below are from *The Secret Diary of Sarah Thomas*, a woman who lived over a hundred years before Zlata. Sarah's diary was discovered and published many years after her death. We discover that Sarah is in love with John, but is not sure that he will be a suitable husband.

> **Mon 18th** This is the day dear J. said he would come. I wanted to go out badly, but didn't want to miss him. What makes it so vexatious is that he didn't come. I opened the green door for him and foolish me, I watched in the summer house for him for a long time.

> **Wed 20th** I ran into the parlour before breakfast and found three letters for me. One in large writing that seemed familiar, so I opened it hastily and found that it was John's. He apologised for not coming on Monday. I read it hastily, devouring his every word and my eye rested on – 'I shall not be coming again as the week following I shall be marrying.' It so upset me I could not read another word as my eyes were filled with tears. Kate could hardly console me. I could not hear her words for some time as I was racked with uncontrolled sobbing. Then she put her arms round me and was laughing as she pointed out that he was marrying a couple the following week and the wedding would delay him for a while.

Think about this. ❂ What details show us the strength of Sarah's feelings? ❂ What does Sarah misunderstand in John's letter? ❂ What do you think John's profession is?

> **Thurs 26th** A lovely day, warm and sunny. Ellen, Kate and John and self walked through the grove and back home by the lodge. I was sadly vexed to discover from their talk that while I was upstairs John had tried to kiss Ellen. I was annoyed with John. He is so light and trifling.

> **Sun 29th** My mind is unsettled still. I think much of dear J. Half inclined to accept him as I feel much pleasure in his company, but shrink from his trifling ways. I went to chapel. There the pulpit was hung all round with black crepe in mourning for Prince Albert [Queen Victoria's husband].

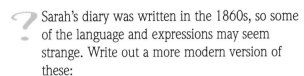

Think about this. ✪ What impression do you gain of John's character? ✪ Do you think Sarah should marry him?

Well, Sarah marries someone else. Here is an extract from her diary entry on her wedding day.

Wed 3rd My bridesmaids were in white grenadine with pink trimming and sashes, with pink and white hawthorn wreaths and tulle veils. They looked really lovely and charming. My own dress, a handsomely worked muslin, with clematis and orange blossom wreath and lace veil.

Sarah's diary was written in the 1860s, so some of the language and expressions may seem strange. Write out a more modern version of these:
(a) I was sadly vexed.
(b) He is so light and trifling.

Choose one day this week and plan your diary entry for that day. Try to show what's going on in your life, and include events, thoughts and comments. Make a Mind Map of your ideas.

WIZARD TIP

You may be asked to write a diary entry for one of your class or exam assignments. Some points to remember:

- You can use note form and abbreviations – but don't overdo them!

- There is no set way of writing a diary – but accuracy and correct spelling are still important.

- Write in the present tense, apart from when you are describing a past event.

section round-up

You have read different kinds of diary, and thought about the way they are written and what we learn from reading them.

Over to you

Each diary entry gives us some idea of what life was like during the period the writer describes. Write in the chart, below, keywords for what you find out.

customs	clothing	private events	public events

Lives

about this section

This section focuses on the different ways in which writers describe their lives and other people's lives. You will think about:

- The differences between biography and autobiography.

- The way writers select incidents to create particular effects.

- How writers use language to shape our ideas about people and their lives.

When someone writes about his or her own life, the work is called **autobiography**. When someone writes about someone else's life, the work is called **biography**. ✪ What are the advantages and disadvantages of people writing their own life stories? What differences might you find between a biography and an autobiography of the same person? Add your ideas to the Mind Map.

Carol singing

Here are two extracts from autobiographies. The first is from *Cider with Rosie*, by Laurie Lee, which describes growing up in the Cotswolds in the 1920s. The second is from *Her People*, by Kathleen Dayfus, which describes growing up in Birmingham in the early 1900s.

1

The week before Christmas, when snow seemed to lie thickest, was the moment for carol-singing; and when I think back to those nights it is to the crunch of snow and to the light of lanterns on it. Steadily we worked through the length of the valley. It was freezing hard and blowing too; yet not for a moment did we feel the cold. Mile after mile we went, fighting against the wind, falling into snowdrifts, and navigating by the lights of the houses. And yet we never saw our audience. We called at house after house; we sang in courtyards and porches, outside windows, or in the damp gloom of hallways; we heard voices from hidden rooms; we smelt rich clothes and strange hot food; we saw maids bearing in dishes or carrying away coffee cups; we received nuts, cakes, figs, preserved ginger, dates, cough-drops, and money; but we never once saw our patrons.

2

The night before this particular Christmas Eve it was snowing and freezing hard when Frankie, Liza and I hurried along the streets to sing carols. Frankie nipped smartly up the baker's entry and helped himself to a large empty flour sack. This was to keep us warm while we waited for the shops to close and the pub across the street to fill with customers. The three of us sat on an empty shop step, huddled up close together with the sack over our heads to keep us warm. Although we were covered in flour we didn't mind as long as we didn't feel the cold.

The lights shone from the leaded window of the George and Dragon. We stood just inside the doorway out of the snow, wiped the snow and flour off our faces, and began to sing. But we couldn't hear ourselves above the noise of merriment going on inside, so Frankie pushed the door open a little and kept his foot there. We waited until the sound had died down, then burst with 'Hark, the Herald Angels Sing'. Someone shouted from inside, 'Some bloody angels!'

'Close the door,' somebody else cried.

This dampened our spirits. Frankie retrieved his foot and we walked away.

Your turn

? How are the writers' carol-singing experiences similar? How are they different?

? Both these writers grew up around the time of the First World War. What details show that the passages describe life in years gone by?

? Pick out words and phrases from either passage that you think are effective. Explain to a friend why you like these expressions.

? Choose a day you celebrate – it might be Christmas, or another festival, or a birthday. Write a description of how you spend the day to include in your autobiography.

WIZARD WORDBOX

You can increase your vocabulary by finding out about the origins of words. *Autobiography* is made up from:

auto = self
bio   = life
graph = write

Complete the chart and add other words you can think of that begin with *auto*, *bio* or *graph*.

word	meaning
automatic	
	study of living things

Different versions

Here are three extracts about the life of Enid Blyton, a popular children's writer whose books were published between the 1940s and the 1960s.

First, read what Enid Blyton said about her own life and work.

When children come to visit me they always want to see two things in my house. They want to see the room where I keep all the books I have ever written, and they want to see my daughters' old nursery. I would take you to see the big bookcase in which I have put all the books I have written. I am always amused when I watch you opening the big glass doors of the bookcase, looking up and down the shelves. If I'm not careful you sit down in a corner and begin to read!

Do you remember Mam'zelle in the St. Clare's school stories? Plump, amusing, hot-tempered, easy to play tricks on? She was one of the French mistresses I had at school. She did many of the things she does in the books. She flew into rages, she stamped and wailed aloud at our stupidity. We played tricks on her. Dear Mam'zelle, she was so easy to take in. She is one of the few people who live on in my books, real and unchanged.

Think about this. ✪ What impression do you get of Enid Blyton's character? ✪ Does she enjoy children's visits to her house? ✪ What do you think about the way she portrays her old French teacher in her books?

This extract is from the autobiography of Enid Blyton's daughter.

Children did arrive at the front door with its big iron bell-pull to see if my mother was in. My mother always came to see them at the door and if she was not too busy, and liked the look of them, she would ask them into the lounge and talk with them. I was a little frightened of these visitors and embarrassed by them. Did they really not know what it was like here? I asked myself. And how was it that they went freely into the lounge, where I was not allowed?

Think about this. ✪ What impression of Enid Blyton's character is given in this extract? ✪ What impression do you get of the relationship between her and her daughter?

Finally, here is a passage adapted from a biography that focuses on Enid Blyton's work and career.

One feature for which Enid Blyton's school stories have been criticized is the use of the French teacher as a butt for practical jokes. Enid Blyton is quite ruthless in the way in which she allows this character to maltreat the English language for humorous effect. The French teacher is at the centre of one of the best comic episodes in the whole of Enid Blyton's work, in *Fifth Formers of St Clare's*, when Mam'zelle believes herself to be on the track of burglars.

Think about this. What is said here about Enid Blyton's portrayal of her old French teacher?

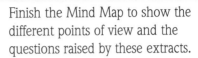
Over to you

Finish the Mind Map to show the different points of view and the questions raised by these extracts.

section round-up

Now you should be able to discuss some different ways of writing about people's lives, and understand the difference between biography and autobiography.

WIZARD READ
You might enjoy some of these lives:
Cider with Rosie by Laurie Lee;
Her People by Kathleen Dayfus;
My Left Foot by Christy Brown;
My Family and Other Animals by Gerald Durrell.

6

Travel

1

about this section

This section will make you familiar with:

- Some different purposes of travel writing.

- Modern and earlier travel writing.

- Different styles of travel writing.

Travel writing can bring to life places we have never visited, and can give us a fresh view of places that are familiar. The Mind Map shows some of the reasons for reading travel literature, and some of the different forms it takes. Copy the map and add your own ideas as you work through the chapter.

African adventures

In the first extract, from *On Foot through Africa*, Ffyona Campbell describes some of her experiences as she walked through Africa. The second extract describes the journeys of an earlier traveller, Mary Kingsley, who also had painful experiences in Africa about a hundred years previously. Her book is called *Travels in West Africa*.

In temperatures of 35C and very high humidity, my upper lip was wet and my clothes sodden before breakfast. Sweat ran down my chest like rain down a window. But there was no breeze to evaporate it and I overheated many times. Little bugs crawled all over my body. They especially seemed to like wriggling in the wetness where my hair grew on my temples and in the sweat on my neck. I couldn't sit still yet was too weary to walk around and shake them off. I wanted to clean myself up; I hadn't had a shower for two days; if I scratched myself, my nails were left thick with black sweaty crud. It was frightening to wake in the night and find I'd been hacking the hell out of the infected sores with dirty nails. I'd thrash around, trying to find a comfortable position where my legs didn't throb from the poison but if I lay still, I could feel dozens of other things which were still on the move – all over my body.

I set off, but bites had swollen my right calf and the outside of my right thigh, restricting the movement of the muscles and making it painful to walk. Worse than the bites themselves, however, was the knowledge that I would be bitten there again during the day. It was not like other illnesses, where at least you know you will get over it. This, having set in, was continuous.

The path went out, but appeared again on the other side of a clump of underbush. I made a short cut for it and the next news was I was in a heap, on a lot of pikes, some fifteen feet or so below ground level, at the bottom of a game pit.

It is at these times you realise the blessing of a good thick skirt. Had I paid heed to the advice of many people in England and adopted masculine garments, I should have been spiked to the bone, and done for. Whereas, save for a good many bruises, here I was with the fullness of my skirt tucked under me, sitting on nine ebony spikes some twelve inches long, in comparative comfort, howling lustily to be hauled out.

We were two hours and a quarter crossing the swamp. One and all, we got horribly infested with leeches. [A leech is a type of worm with suckers at each end. It attaches itself to the body and shrivels if salt is thrown on it.] Knowing you do not like my going into details on such matters, I will confine my statement regarding our leeches, to the fact that it was for the best that we had some salt with us. It was most comic to see us salting each other, but in spite of the salt's action I was quite faint from loss of blood. The bleeding did not stop at once, and it attracted flies and – but I am going into details, so I forbear.

Try this

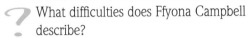

What difficulties does Ffyona Campbell describe?

Underline words that show her discomfort and pain.

Why were the infected bites worse than other illnesses?

What two separate incidents does Mary Kingsley describe?

What advice had she been given about how to dress? Why was she glad that she had not taken that advice?

What differences and similarities do you find in the writers' accounts? The Mind Map gives you some prompts. Add your own ideas.

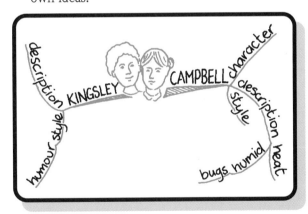

What differences do you find in the way the writers express themselves? Find some examples for the following points, and think of more headings.

1994 account	1897 account
Fairly short sentences e.g:	Some long sentences e.g:
Colloquial expressions e.g: hacking the hell	

WIZARD WORDBOX

The word *colloquial* refers to the kind of language we use in conversation. It is made up from:

col = with
loqui = speak

Another word root that indicates speech is *logo*.

✪ Think of words to do with speaking that are derived from *loqui* or *logo*. Here are a couple to start you off: *elocution; monologue*

Come to Cuba

Here are four extracts from writing about Havana, the capital of Cuba. The first is by the nineteenth-century novelist, Anthony Trollope, and the second is by the television presenter Clive Anderson. These are followed by two guide-book extracts.

Trollope describes his experiences of Havana hotels.

I found it impossible to command the luxury of a bedroom to myself. It was not the custom of the country, they told me. If I chose to pay five dollars a day, just double the usual price, I could be indulged as soon as circumstances would admit of it; which was intended to signify that they would be happy to charge me for the second bed as soon as the time should come that they had no-one else on whom to levy the rate. And the dirt of that bedroom!

I complained somewhat bitterly to an American acquaintance, who had as I thought been more lucky in his inn.

'One companion!' said he. 'Why, I have three. One walks about all night in a bed-gown, a second snores, and the other is dying!'

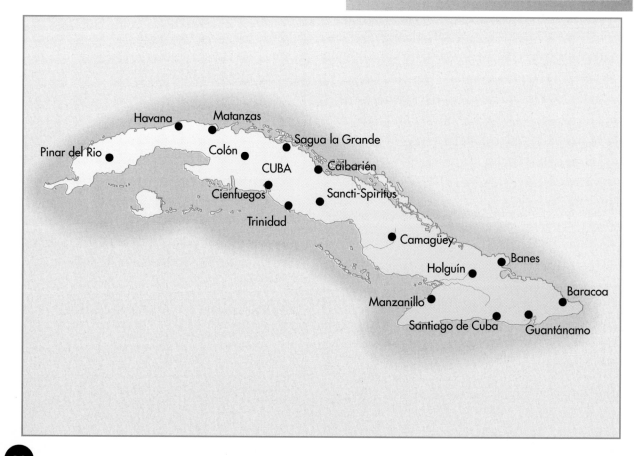

Clive Anderson describes shopping in Havana.

2

The average Cuban queues up not only to get on a bus, but also to buy goods in a shop, when they are available. Basic foodstuffs are rationed. Shops for the average Cuban are dreary counters where your allowance of rice and cooking is doled out to you. In one shop I went into, only one product was displayed on the shelves – tins of dull-looking beans. I commiserated with the shopkeeper. It was a shame that was all she had to sell. Actually, she explained, things were worse than that. The tins were empty. They were just there for decoration.

3

Havana is located to one side of a huge bay on Cuba's north coast. The name invokes the whiff of a Cuban cigar, the mellow tang of aged rum. It is only by exploring its intimate corners, broad boulevards, fine promenade and old quarter, that you can begin to appreciate the complexity of this ancient city and the surprises it has to offer. It is like no other city in the world, a place where soaring skyscraper blocks rub shoulders with dilapidated villas and town houses.

4

This is one of Havana's premier hotels. It is handily situated and reasonably priced. There is a great view to be had from the top floor roof-terrace, but you will need to cough up $3 to get in (you do get a cocktail thrown in with the price). The ground floor cafeteria serves the most unappetising and over-priced pizzas in Cuba. The dollar shop in the hotel stocks the most extensive array of gifts in the city. A set of tacky maracas will cost you $6 while a wall-mounted crab is a pinch at $5.

6

Your turn

Here are some reminders of aspects of the content and style of the extracts. Use arrows to put each suggestion in the appropriate box or boxes. Add your own ideas to the list.

Trollope (1)

Anderson (2)

scarcity of food

poor food

sharing bedrooms ←

the variety of the city

expensive food

sense of the romance of the city

favourable adjectives

Guide (3)

humour.

Guide (4)

purpose: tourist information

purpose: to inspire

personal anecdote [short account of something that has happened to the writer]

colloquial language

Prepare a short talk about a place you know well. You can be critical, complimentary or both. You could record your talk and ask a friend for feedback.

 After all that travelling you deserve a break!

section round-up

You've shown that you can understand different examples of travel writing, and can identify features of content and style. Well done!

WIZARD READ

You may enjoy these travel books: *Boogie Down the River* by Mark Wallington; *The Virago Book of Women Travellers*, edited by Mary Morris.

Information

about this section

This section will give you practice in:

- Selecting information.
- Presenting information for a particular purpose.

As you know, information comes in many forms, including such aspects as facts, comments, statistics, examples. Handling information is an important part of your English course and is, of course, an essential life skill as well! In all kinds of situations it is important to be able to give clear information in an appropriate form, and to be able to select the information you need.

WIZARD WORDBOX

At the top of this page you are told you will get 'practice' in selecting information. Remember the difference between **practice** and **practise**. **Practice** is a noun – it's the name of something. **Practise** is a verb – it describes an action. You could remember the difference by thinking of the 's' in practise as standing for sport – something you **do**.

Pain in the neck

Here is lots of **information** about school students and neck and back pain. It's presented in a variety of forms. First, read all the information.

My back and neck really ache!

You shouldn't carry your bag around all day.

I have to – we haven't got lockers.

Report from National Back Pain Association

By the age of 14, more than 50% of children will be suffering from back discomfort.

80% of schoolchildren surveyed are carrying badly designed bags or carrying them incorrectly.

Some children are carrying more than a third of their body weight in their school bags.

The risks are highest with younger secondary school children especially when carrying the weekly extra items, such as sports gear.

92% of pupils surveyed state that their school did not encourage bags to be carried with both shoulders.

The average bag weight is 5.5kg and 7.5kg with extra kit.

The maximum recommended weight for a 14 year old is 10.4% of body weight. The National Back Pain Association has a target of 5.2% of body weight.

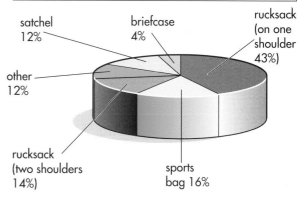

satchel 12%

briefcase 4%

rucksack (on one shoulder 43%)

other 12%

rucksack (two shoulders 14%)

sports bag 16%

Bag design and carrying methods

Satchels or rucksacks with two thick straps should be used and carried on both shoulders at all times. If this isn't possible, they should be carried with both arms close to the body.

Lifting bags on to the back at the end of lessons should be attempted by placing the bag on the table with the straps hanging over the front edge of the desk. Children can then turn round, bend at the knees, loop their arms through and stand with the load evenly distributed on the back. This avoids bags being swung on to the back – a potential source of injury in the class.

6

Task time

Your task is to prepare a talk for parents in your year group on the subject 'Are school bags a health hazard we should be doing something about?'
Select the information you want to use.
Draw a Mind Map to plan your talk. Record your talk – or you could ask your teacher if you can practise it in front of your class.
If you prefer, you could design a leaflet.

I suppose I could carry just one file with what I need for the day.

We could try to timetable sport and practical lessons on different days.

section round-up

Well done! You've shown you can read information a variety of forms and use it for a particular purpose.

SPELL-BINDING

To work some memory magic, remind yourself of what you've learnt. If you've been adding to a chapter Mind Map, review it now. Then try the checklist below.

Answers to 'Try this' (p. 63)
1C, 2K, 3J, 4A, 5B, 6G, 7F, 8I, 9H, 10E

Answers

checklist

Could you now:

	Yes	Not yet
1 Understand what is meant by purpose in non-fiction writing? (p. 64)	◯	◯
2 Explain what is meant by audience in non-fiction writing? (p. 64)	◯	◯
3 Set out a personal letter? (p. 69)	◯	◯
4 Set out a business letter? (p. 69)	◯	◯
5 Explain what we can learn from reading other people's letters? (pp. 66–8)	◯	◯
6 Describe the difference between biography and autobiography? (p. 74)	◯	◯
7 Identify some of the differences in language use in earlier periods? (p. 79)	◯	◯
8 Explain how different accounts of the same subject can vary? (pp. 80–1)	◯	◯
9 Describe some of the techniques writers use to achieve their purpose? (p. 82)	◯	◯

If your answer to any of these questions is 'Not yet', look back at the pages shown. If you're still unsure, ask your teacher for help.

The media

overview

This chapter is about the media – including newspapers, magazines, radio and television. It will tell you about:

- The difference between facts and opinions.
- Bias and emotive language.
- The use of words and pictures to persuade.
- How advertising works.
- Magazines and who reads them.
- Differences between the media.

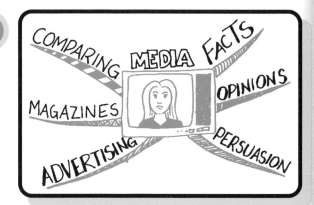

- A woodlouse remembers for two seconds.
- Chocolate contains more sugar than celery.

Opinions are points of view or judgements. Here are some opinions:

- Arsenal is the greatest football team of all time.
- People who smoke must be mad.
- Children should be seen and not heard.

Getting your facts wrong

It is possible to get facts wrong, or even to tell a deliberate lie, yet still make a factual **statement**:

> *Zebras are pink with blue spots.*

Facts, opinions and bias

about this section

This section explains the difference between facts and opinions, and how bias and emotive language can affect our view of the facts.

Facts in the media

Newspapers contain a mixture of **facts** and **opinions**. These two things are explained below.

Facts are generally accepted as true and can be proven. Here are some facts:

- King Harold the Great was killed by an arrow in his eye.

Confused facts

Our research assistant has got the facts below mixed up. ✪ Match up the halves of each confused factual statement to turn them into correct facts.

Madrid is the capital of	the home.
Chimpanzees and gorrillas	drive on the wrong side of the road.
Anteaters	can kick a ball very accurately.
Bart Simpson is	President of the United States.
It is against the law to	eat a lot of fruit.
Abraham Lincoln used to be	a cartoon character.
Most minor accidents happen in	Spain.
Professional footballers	have long tongues.

Bias

Referees are supposed to make fair decisions.
The referee shown here is guilty of **bias**:

News reporting can also be biased. This bias can be
unconscious or **conscious**. Unconscious bias is
when a reporter does not realise that a comment is
biased. Conscious bias is deliberate. Reporters are
sometimes deliberately biased because the
newspaper or broadcasting company they work for
supports one political party or one viewpoint.

There are four main types of bias in news reporting:

1 **Interpretation**: explaining events in a way that
   supports a particular opinion.
2 **Selection**: reporting only those facts that support
   a particular opinion.
3 **Exaggeration**: making something seem much
   better or worse than it really is.
4 **Emotive language**: choosing words that will stir
   up people's emotions – which will, in turn, affect
   what they think.

The news reports below contain examples of all four types of bias. One is from a paper that supports the National Alliance Party, the other from a paper that does not.

Notice:

- how figures are used;
- the words 'gangs' and 'prowling'. Also notice the picture and its caption.

BAGTHORPE HERALD

CRIME WAVE OUT OF CONTROL

The Government Minister for Law and Order, David Stone, today tried to explain away figures showing that crime has soared in the last six months. Crime is now completely out of control. There were 4,800 unsolved burglaries last month alone. People dare not leave their homes unguarded for fear that gangs of prowling youths will break in. Critics of the government say tough new measures are needed ...

A nervous David Stone puts on a brave face for the cameras.

DAILY COMET

CRIME POLICY PAYS OFF

The Government Minister for Law and Order, David Stone, has welcomed figures showing that confidence in the police is at an all-time high. The public now considers almost all crimes worth reporting. Arrests have increased and out of 25,000 burglaries nationwide last month – the lowest figure in three years – only 4,800 remained unsolved. He also praised the successes of Neighbourhood Watch schemes.

A delighted David Stone welcomes new crime figures.

Task time

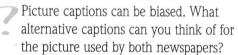

Did you manage to put together the correct facts from p. 85? When you think you've got them right, think of one opinion about each subject. Example: 'Abraham Lincoln was a great man.'

Sort the following into facts and opinions (answers at end of chapter):
  A Water never flows uphill.
  B Torquay is a holiday resort with something for everyone.
  C The steam engine was the most important invention of the eighteenth century.
  D Water expands when it freezes.
  E Education is the key to success.
  F All accidents are avoidable.

Copy or underline any examples of bias you find in the two newspaper articles. Then read the front page of a real newspaper and underline any possible bias you find.

Picture captions can be biased. What alternative captions can you think of for the picture used by both newspapers?

Watch a television news broadcast. Note at least three facts, two opinions and one example of possible bias.

section round-up

You should by now understand the difference between facts and opinions. You should also be able to explain the meaning of bias, give examples of it and begin to notice it in reporting.

Take a break – or you may need some persuasion to start the next section.

7

Persuasion

about this section

Read this section and you will find out about using words and pictures to persuade.

Persuasion – what it is and how to do it

Persuasion means getting someone to do something – or not do it. The examples below and opposite show both types. Leaflets and posters use words and pictures together to persuade.

What sort?

Before choosing an animal think about your lifestyle and where you live. Cats and dogs like to spend time outside – do you have a secure garden? It doesn't make sense to have a dog if you live in a high-rise flat, or cats if you live on a busy road. Do you work or have a baby, young children or an elderly person living with you? It's also important to think well into the future – are you sure that you will be able to give your animal a good home for perhaps 15 years? Remember too that animals need different levels of exercise and have very different temperaments. If space is limited at home, don't have the first cute mongrel puppy you see – it could be part Great Dane!

time! If you're overly house-proud then don't get a dog or cat; their hairs can get everywhere, some never stop chewing furniture or climbing up curtains, even if they have toys and scratching posts, and they can become quite smelly as they get older! It's also no good being squeamish, you may need to worm your animal, treat it for fleas or other problems and clear up after it. Having a pet is not just **your** decision. Discuss it with all members of your household and make sure everyone agrees before you commit yourself. And never take an animal on out of pity. To take on a friend's unwanted dog is not helping it if you do not have the space, time or money to care for it.

Why do you want a pet?

Before you get a pet, think carefully about why you want an animal. Owning a pet is great fun but remember if it is ill, you must take it to the vet; if you go on holiday, you must make sure it is properly looked after. And pets aren't lovely all the

NHPA/GERARD LACZ

NHPA/GERARD LACZ

RSPCA/D MUSCROFT

RSPCA/SUSAN PITTS

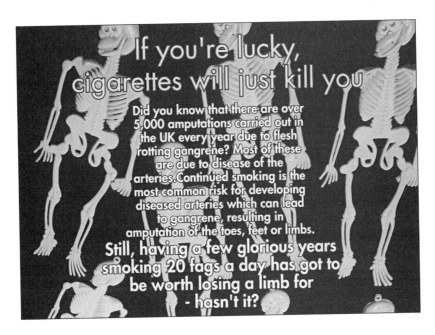

If you're lucky, cigarettes will just kill you

Did you know that there are over 5,000 amputations carried out in the UK every year due to flesh rotting gangrene? Most of these are due to disease of the arteries. Continued smoking is the most common risk for developing diseased arteries which can lead to gangrene, resulting in amputation of the toes, feet or limbs. Still, having a few glorious years smoking 20 fags a day has got to be worth losing a limb for - hasn't it?

Most persuasive writing contains three things:

1 **Information** – it is important to give the right amount.
2 **Argument** – the reasons: they need to work on the people you hope to persuade.
3 **Instruction** – telling people what they should do and how they should do it.

Here are some persuasive techniques to look for in the examples on this page and on page 88 and to try out:

- Get readers on your side – start with something they will agree with.
- Humour – wins people over and makes them remember your message.
- Emotional appeal – if people feel pity, anger, fear or guilt, this may make them act.
- Questions and answers – this gets people involved.

Try this

 Use Mind Maps or lists to summarise the information given by each example.

 Look at the illustrations in the examples. Which approach is gentle? Which aims to shock? What pictures could the RSPCA use instead to show

what happens when people buy pets without thinking? What pictures could Quit use to show the benefits of not smoking?

Try to persuade a partner to do something that would be good for them, or give up something that is bad for them. Your partner must let you talk for two minutes.

The Quit material focuses on one reason for not smoking. Mind Map or list as many others as you can think of. Then design an anti-smoking leaflet using one or more of your reasons.

section round-up

You should now understand how persuasive materials use information, argument and instruction. You should also know some of the techniques used. From now on, keep a look out for them. If you think you can now spot some of them, well done!

STOP   You look tired: can we persuade you to take a break?

7

Advertising

about this section

This section is about a special type of persuasion – advertising. You will learn about how advertisements get our attention, what makes us remember them and how they appeal to a particular market.

Pay attention!

The first thing advertisements have to do is GRAB OUR ATTENTION! They may use:

* shock
* something funny or ridiculous
* sex and romance
* exciting music
* bright colours
* a famous person.

Different things work on different sorts of buyer.
✪ What works on you?

Remember me?

Advertisers must make us remember their product long enough to buy it. Anything that catches our attention is a good start. Other things that help are:

* Stories – easiest on television or radio.
* Slogans – clever-sounding, catchy phrases, often using a pun (double meaning).
* Jingles – slogans set to music.

Advertisers also try to persuade us by listing the product's selling points, producing 'evidence', or tempting us with promises and special offers.

Now look at the advertisements in this section. ✪ How do they get our attention? What makes them easy to remember? What techniques of persuasion do they use?

THE WEST END'S
"MONSTER HIT"
DAILY MIRROR

ROBERT STIGWOOD
PAUL NICHOLAS & DAVID IAN
PRESENT

LUKE GOSS as DANNY

"IT'S THE ONE THAT YOU WANT!"

"A SMASH HIT"
DAILY MAIL

Tuesday 5th May -Saturday 6th June
EVENINGS AT 7.30PM. MATINEES ON WED & SAT AT 2.30PM
Tickets: £7.00-£24.50 Concessions available

ALL THE UNFORGETTABLE SONGS FROM THE HIT FILM:
SUMMER NIGHTS ● HOPELESSLY
DEVOTED TO YOU ● GREASE IS THE WORD
SANDY ● GREASED LIGHTNIN'
YOU'RE THE ONE THAT I WANT & many more!

Packed with explosive energy, this
multi-million £££s high octane rock
and roll party is THE MOST ELECTRIFYING
EXTRAVAGANZA IN TOWN.

MAKE SURE THAT YOU DON'T MISS
THE BEST PARTY IN TOWN!

Think you're smart?

? Keep an advertising diary for a typical day. Note the different types advertising 'medium' – for example, billboards. At the end of the day, list them. Note how advertisements vary from one type of medium to another – for example, the back of a bus and a magazine.

? Which techniques can you identify in the advertisements in this section? Can you find a pun in the 'Bungie' advertisement? What is the *Grease* advertisement's slogan?

? If there is a product that you like or want, then you are part of its market. Design an advertisement aimed at the same market – at young people like you.

section round-up

You should now understand some of the techniques of advertising. To learn more, look out for them every time you watch a television commercial break or pass a billboard poster.

 Time for a break – maybe there's a Bungie bar in the house!

7

Magazines

What is a magazine?

The word *magazine* comes from an Arabic word for a 'storehouse'. Magazines are storehouses of entertainment and information. Some are of general interest, while others are for readers with special interests. Large newsagents sell magazines covering dozens of interests.

Target audience

Most magazines are aimed at an exact group of people – for example, not just people who like pop music, but people aged 16–21 who like a particular type of pop music, dress in a certain way and have £2.50 a week to spend on a magazine.

Practice time

Look at the magazine shown here. Who do you think it is aimed at? What kind of **regulars** (appearing every issue) and **features** (one-offs) would you expect it to have?

Buy or borrow a magazine that looks interesting but which you have not read before. What regulars and features does it have? What advertisements? Is it written in a particular style? Describe its **target audience**.

Write the Contents page of your own ideal magazine.

section round-up

This section has told you about magazines and their target audiences. Next time you go into a newsagent, notice how many different types of magazine there are.

Comparing media

about this section

This section compares the presentation of news in three different media: newspapers, television and radio.

You may think the news is the same whatever form it comes in. In fact, what we are told varies depending on the **medium** – newspapers, television or radio. Take two minutes to think about the differences. Jot down or Mind Map your thoughts.

Now check your ideas against the following list of differences:

- **Newspapers** have words and still photographs. They can use more words because people can read at their own speed, or miss bits out. News stories may be a day old if an event occurs just after they have been printed – but some newspapers have news websites updated hourly. They may focus on stories that they think will sell more copies of the paper.

- **Television** has words and moving pictures, but it takes time to get a reporter and camera crew to the scene of an event. Television has to entertain viewers, so producers spend more time on stories offering exciting or interesting pictures.

- **Radio** only has sound, but it is the most immediate news medium. A reporter with a mobile phone can be on the scene very quickly, and there are regular updates. Listeners can tune in when in their cars.

Now read the *Guardian* newspaper story below. It is about the capture of the second of two pigs who escaped death in an abattoir (where animals are killed for meat). The pigs escaped by wriggling under a fence and swimming a river. When you have finished, Mind Map the main points.

Tamworth One cops it in copse, ending great escape

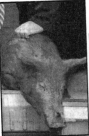

The Sundance Pig, back in custody after week on run

Geoffrey Gibbs

AFTER more than a week on the run the Sundance Pig was not going to come quietly. His partner might have been captured, but the porker that got away was determined to enjoy his last moments of freedom.

For hours again yesterday he frustrated police officers, RSPCA inspectors, dog handlers and a watching army of 100 journalists and camera crews by hiding in a dense thicket of brambles at Tet-bury Hill, Malmesbury, in Wiltshire.

Flushed out at last by a spaniel named Pepsi, the fugitive scampered across a field to a copse before turning to face the inevitable tranquilliser gun.

Even then he was not going to make it easy. Twice the anaesthetic-laden darts bounced off his hide. But as RSPCA inspector Mike Harley fired for a third time the pig's movements slowed.

A "snout grabber" was placed over his head to restrain his movements. The pig's days on the run were over.

Last night the youthful young Ginger Tamworth boar, who escaped from the town's slaughterhouse with a female companion, was resting in a veterinary hospital's recovery pen. "It's an ordinary healthy pig." said Mr Harley. "I am very glad that we caught it today and that it is a happy ending."

Vets and the Daily Mail, which now claims ownership of the two pigs, were taking no chances that an animal described by police as "cunning and devious" would repeat his escape.

Sundance — groggy but back on his feet — was being held in a chained and padlocked pen behind 6ft high gates. Vet Fran Baird expected the boar to make a full recovery but said it would remain at the hospital for a day or so.

Once recovered the boar will be taken to the Langley Wild Animal Rescue Sanctuary, near Chippenham, where owners Kevin and Debbie Stinchcombe are already looking after Sundance's companion — the pig formerly renamed Tammy.

Debate

Debate is organised discussion. All three media have debate, but it is more difficult in newspapers than on television or radio. Radio phone-ins like the one on this page make public debate possible.

✪ Why would they work less well on television?

The *Guardian* article on this page is about the escaped pigs you read about on the previous page. It offers quite light-hearted **debate** on the subject. See what two contradictory views of pigs the writer identifies. Note: **synonyms for** means 'words meaning the same thing as'; **porcine** means 'in the form of a pig'; **immortalised** means 'enabled to live for ever'.

Love the piggy within
For they are just like us

WE eat almost every bit of them — except the squeal — with their meat more variously named than any other species: gammon, ham, bacon and, of course, pork. They are the subjects of nursery rhymes (This little piggy. . .), children's stories (Three Little Pigs) and everyday metaphor (piggy in the middle). They have been the pets of a premier (Stanley Baldwin) and the object of obsessive love (remember Lord Emsworth's passion for his prize porker, the Empress of Blandings?) This week they became the object of that ever-so-British phenomenon: a bout of collective, animal-inspired madness. The Guardian cannot tell the inside story of the Tamworth Two's flight from the slaughterhouse — that's been bought up for £15,000 by the Daily Mail. That newspaper now has some explaining to do. What message has it sent to the 15 million other pigs sentenced to the abattoir each year: escape from pig-jail and your defiance shall be rewarded with a life of peace and animal sanctuary? The Daily Mail's long record on law and order must now be called into question.

The task now is to sort out what is clearly a relationship of deep, but mixed emotions: the British and the Pig. On the one hand, we use them as synonyms for dirt and crudity. The unevolved man is a "male chauvinist pig", while, to those wary of police heavy-handedness, the constabulary are "the pigs". Literature has cast them as frequent villains — most famously in the form of Napoleon, the porcine dictator of Animal Farm. We chop up all their bits for food with barely a squeal of dissent.

And yet we cherish our pink friends. A A Milne's Piglet is a cutie, Miss Piggy a favourite Muppet. Now Butch and Sundance are to join the porker hall of fame, immortalised as a pair of soft toys — coming in "beige-pink colour with soft ears and likely to sell for under £10 each". Perhaps the stand-out, though, was Babe — the precursor of the Tamworth duo in its plucky determination to dodge its fate. It is no coincidence that pigs are often used as a substitute for humans in films, scientific experiments and the like. For our attitude to pigs is the same as our view of humans: we don't know whether to love them or hate them.

Radio phone-in

Presenter: And we have a caller in Wiltshire on the line. Joy Alan.

Joy Alan: I'm a vegetarian, and I think this story highlights the fact that we shouldn't be eating these animals in the first place. I'm glad they escaped, but it doesn't save the other poor pigs, cows and sheep murdered every year ...

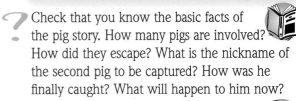

Tasks

? Check that you know the basic facts of the pig story. How many pigs are involved? How did they escape? What is the nickname of the second pig to be captured? How was he finally caught? What will happen to him now?

? Continue the radio phone-in as a discussion with one or more friends. One of you should be the presenter. Introduce someone who thinks vegetarianism is stupid.

? Plan a television news story on the pig's capture. Write it as a storyboard or script (including descriptions of film pictures). Include:
(a) the newsreader at the newsdesk;
(b) the reporter at the scene;
(c) an interview with two of the following – the RSPCA officer, a police officer, the abattoir owner, Kevin or Debbie Stinchcombe.

section round-up

You should now know what the main media are, and what their advantages and disadvantages are in presenting and debating news.

SPELL-BINDING

To work some memory magic, remind yourself now of what you've learnt. If you've been making a chapter Mind Map, check it against the Mind Map on this page. Then try the checklist.

Answers

checklist

Could you now:

	Yes	Not yet
1 Explain the difference between facts and opinions? (p. 85)	◯	◯
2 Find examples of bias in newspapers? (p. 86)	◯	◯
3 Look at a leaflet and say how it informs or persuades readers? (pp. 88–9)	◯	◯
4 Spot at least two sales techniques in magazine or television advertising? (p. 90)	◯	◯
5 Name two magazines and describe their target audience? (p. 92)	◯	◯
6 List advantages and disadvantages of news presentation in different media? (p. 93)	◯	◯

If your answer to any of these questions is 'Not yet', look back at the pages shown. If you're still unsure, ask your teacher for help.

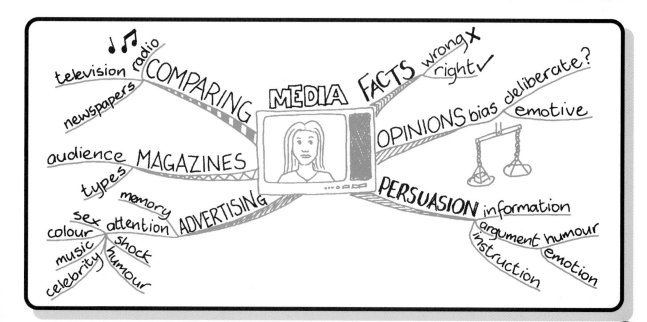

Shakespeare

overview

Worried about understanding Shakespeare? Or just keen to find out more? Here's what you'll discover in this chapter:

- Who Shakespeare was and what the theatre was like in his day.

- What kinds of plays he wrote and how to enjoy them.

- How to get to grips with Shakespeare's characters.

- How to understand and appreciate his language.

- How to enjoy and comment on a Shakespeare performance.

Shakespeare and his plays

about this section

This section introduces Shakespeare the man, and Elizabethan theatre. It also tells you about the main types of play Shakespeare wrote. Finally, it explains how a Shakespeare play is structured and how to find your way into a scene.

Meet Shakespeare

Shakespeare was a country boy, though he went to grammar school and read plays and poems in Latin. When he grew up he moved to London, where there were more opportunities for a young playwright. He joined a group of actors, played small parts and started to write plays.

> I was born in Stratford-on-Avon, Warwickshire, in 1564. My father made and sold gloves, so I met all kinds of people.

The Elizabethan theatre

Shakespeare became famous during the reign of Queen Elizabeth I, so we call him an Elizabethan. He wrote his plays not to be read, but to be performed and enjoyed in the theatre. Some were performed before the Queen herself.

You might think the theatre is 'posh', but it wasn't like that in Shakespeare's time. Lords and ladies went to see his plays, but so did people who couldn't read or write. Theatres were circular and open to the sky. The rich sat under shelter round the edge, while the poor stood in front of the stage. Shakespeare had to make his plays enjoyable for the educated and uneducated alike. The actors had to put up with the audience eating, drinking beer and wandering about – even throwing things or shouting to hear the best bits again!

Curtain time

'Curtain time' in a modern theatre means the play is about to start. In an Elizabethan theatre, there were no curtains! There wasn't much scenery either, or special lighting effects, and the costumes had to be used for lots of different parts. The magic of theatre had to be created by words and acting – plus some music to help fix the mood.

Another difference was that in Elizabethan theatre women's parts were acted by boys!

Comedy, tragedy, history

You are probably studying one of three types of Shakespeare play:

- **Comedies** – featuring humour, disguise (especially women dressed as men), trickery, lovesick lovers, happy endings with marriages.
- **Tragedies** – with disagreements and misunderstandings, fights, heroes (and sometimes heroines) who are brave but die in the end.
- **Histories** – based on real historical events and people.

✪ In what ways does the play you are studying fit any of these descriptions?

Acts, scenes and stage directions

Every Shakespeare play is divided into five **Acts**. An Act is like a chapter in a novel. Act 1 introduces the main characters and the basis of the plot. In Act 5 battles are lost and won and peace is restored, or misunderstandings are finally sorted out.

Acts are split into **scenes**. Each scene occurs in a single place. The place itself may add to the mood. In *A Midsummer Night's Dream* love and magic take place in the forest, more down-to-earth things in Athens.

Stage directions say where the scene is, what characters are there and when they **enter** or **exit**.

Getting to grips with a scene

Think your way into a scene by asking yourself questions – perhaps the same questions that Shakespeare asked himself as he wrote the scene:

Task time

❓ Copy the Mini Mind Map opposite. Add to it as you go through the chapter. Compare your growing Mind Map with the full Mind Map at the end.

❓ Write down ten questions you would like to ask Shakespeare in an interview, and ten things you would probably have to explain to him if he spent a day with you.

Try a scene

Here is the start of a scene from *Macbeth*. Banquo, a good man, is with his young son Fleance. Banquo feels heavy with tiredness, yet he is restless and anxious about what thoughts may come when he tries to sleep. The 'candles' he speaks of are the stars. 'Largess' means presents, and 'offices' are servants' quarters.

Act 2, scene 1 *The courtyard of Macbeth's castle. Enter BANQUO and FLEANCE, with a SERVANT bearing a torch before them.*

Banquo: How goes the night, boy?
Fleance: The moon is down; I have not heard the clock.
Banquo: And she goes down at twelve.
Fleance: I take 't, 'tis later, sir.
Banquo: Hold, take my sword. There's husbandry in heaven;
Their candles are all out. Take thee that too.
A heavy summons lies like lead upon me,
And yet I would not sleep: merciful powers,
Restrain in me the cursed thoughts that nature
Gives way to in repose.

Enter MACBETH and a SERVANT with a torch

Give me my sword.
Who's there?
Macbeth: A friend.
Banquo: What, sir! not at rest? The king's a-bed:
He hath been in unusual pleasure, and
Sent forth great largess to your offices.
This diamond he greets your wife withal,
By the name of most kind hostess; and shut up
In measureless content.

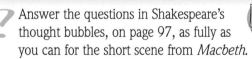

Try this

? Answer the questions in Shakespeare's thought bubbles, on page 97, as fully as you can for the short scene from *Macbeth*.

? Thinking again of the scene from *Macbeth*, imagine it being performed in the Elizabethan theatre at night. Make notes or a Mini Mind Map on what it would be like.

? If you are already studying a Shakespeare play, note down what features make it a comedy, a tragedy or a history. Then read a single scene and use the Shakespeare thought bubbles to help you write notes about it.

? Read the scene aloud, alone or with two friends.

section round-up

If you've paid attention, then you already know a lot about:
• Shakespeare and the Elizabethan theatre.
• Three types of Shakespeare play.
• Acts, scenes and stage directions.
• Asking questions to get into a scene.

Take a break before getting to grips with character.

Getting into character

FIRST IMPRESSIONS – A WIZARD TIP

When you first meet someone, you form an opinion of that person based on the things listed on the left, and what they look like. Even their name may play a part. (What about 'Belch' and 'Aguecheek'?) A playscript does not say much about the characters' appearance, so use your imagination. Try sketching them as you think they would look.

What makes this character tick?

There are four main ways in which we find out about Shakespeare's characters:

1 what they do
2 what they say
3 what others say about them
4 what kind of language they use.

Number 2 (what they say) can be split into what they say:

- **to** others (You're wonderful ...)
- **about** others (She's wonderful ...)
- **about** themselves (I'm wonderful ...).

Meet Sir Toby and Maria

The passage on page 100 is from *Twelfth Night* (Act 1, scene 3). It introduces two characters: Sir Toby Belch and Maria. They are in the house of a wealthy lady, Olivia, whose brother has recently died. Sir Toby is her uncle, Maria is her servant.

The notes on the left explain difficult language. The notes on the right are about the characters. First read the passage aloud with all the notes covered up. Then read it looking at the left-hand notes. Record your impressions of Sir Toby and Maria in two Mini Mind Maps. Then read the notes on the right and add to your Mind Maps.

'Why on earth does my niece take her brother's death so badly?'

ill: late

TOBY: What a plague means my niece to take the death of her brother thus? I am sure care's an enemy of life.

Not very sympathetic. He's a carefree type himself.

MARIA: By my troth, Sir Toby, you must come in earlier of nights: your cousin, my lady, takes great exception to your ill hours.

TOBY: Why, let her except, before excepted.

He doesn't care.

MARIA: Ay, but you must confine yourself within the modest limits of order.

She is firm with him.

TOBY: Confine? I'll confine myself no finer than I am. These clothes are good enough to drink in, and so be these boots too: and they be not, let them hang themselves in their own straps.

He likes word-play. He pretends to misunderstand confine as meaning to 'dress in finery'.

MARIA: That quaffing and drinking will undo you: I heard my lady talk of it yesterday; and of a foolish knight that you brought in one night here to be her wooer.

wooer: lover

TOBY: Who, Sir Andrew Aguecheek?

MARIA: Ay, he.

'What's that got to do with it?'

TOBY: He's as tall a man as any's in Illyria.

MARIA: What's that to the purpose?

His income

TOBY: Why he has three thousand ducats a year.

prodigal: waster

MARIA: Ay, but he'll have but a year in all these ducats. He's a very fool, and a prodigal.

She knows a fool when she sees one.

viol-de-gamboys: a kind of musical instrument

TOBY: Fie, that you'll say so! he plays o' the viol-de-gamboys, and speaks four languages word for word without book, and hath all the good gifts of nature.

MARIA: He hath indeed all, most natural: for besides that he's a fool, he's a great quareller; and but that he hath the gift of a coward to allay the gust he hath in quarelling, 'tis thought among the prudent he would

die ———— quickly have the gift of a grave.

Now she plays with words: natural also meant 'idiot'.

TOBY: By this hand, they are scoundrels and substractors that say so of him. Who are they?

Stands up for his friend.

MARIA: They that add, moreover, he's drunk nightly in your company.

Illyria: imaginary place where play is set.

coistrel: peasant

TOBY: With drinking healths to my niece: I'll drink to her as long as there is a passage in my throat, and drink in Illyria: he's a coward and a coistrel that will not drink to my niece till his brains turn o' the toe, like a parish top. What, wench! *Castiliano vulgo*: for here comes Sir Andrew Agueface.

Thinks highly of Olivia, but also likes an excuse to drink.

Castiliano vulgo: uncertain meaning; possibly 'Hush now!'

How Shakespeare's characters develop

Teachers and examiners will probably ask you to concentrate on a scene, or several scenes. However, to say what a character is really like, you need to understand how the scenes fit into the whole play. Read the play if you can. At least learn the storyline.

Most of the important characters **develop**. Some learn from mistakes and become better people. But not all: Lady Macbeth, for example, goes mad and kills herself.

In *Twelfth Night*, Sir Toby Belch is too much of a drunken rogue to change much, but there is a hint that he learns a lesson when a trick backfires on him. He also marries Maria. In the passage below (Act 2, scene 3), they plan to trick Malvolio into thinking that Olivia loves him, by forging letters from Olivia. Sir Andrew Aguecheek joins in.

The notes on the left explain difficult language. Add to your Mini Mind Maps of Sir Toby and Maria. Begin one on Sir Andrew. Before you start, look back at the beginning of this section to remind yourself of what to watch out for.

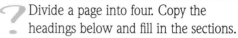

Test your skills

? Divide a page into four. Copy the headings below and fill in the sections.

What Sir Toby says about Sir Andrew	What Maria says about Sir Andrew
What this tells us about Sir Toby	What this tells us about Maria

? You must give **evidence** when you write about characters. Use short quotations, or sum up what they say. The lines with notes on character in the extract opposite could be used as evidence. Underline evidence in the second extract that: (a) Maria thinks Sir Andrew is stupid; (b) All three think it will be fun to trick Malvolio; (c) Toby and Sir Andrew like and respect Maria; (d) Toby is sure of Maria's affection; (e) Sir Andrew's love-life is not going well; (f) Toby sponges money off Sir Andrew.

? Use colours to mark the words below describing (a) Sir Toby, (b) Maria, (c) both. Describe each character, with evidence.

clever   drunken   loyal   fun-loving   sensible   mischievous   playful   quarrelsome

---

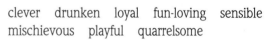

<u>device</u>: trick	TOBY:	Excellent, I smell a device.
	ANDREW:	I have't in my nose too.
	TOBY:	He shall think by the letters that thou will drop that they come from my niece, and that she's in love with him.
'That's the idea.'	MARIA:	My purpose is indeed a horse of that colour.
	ANDREW:	And your horse now would make him an ass.
Agrees, but also calling Andrew an ass.	MARIA:	Ass, I doubt not.
	ANDREW:	O, 'twill be admirable!
	MARIA:	Sport royal, I warrant you: I know my physic will work with him. I will plant you two, and let the fool make a third, where he shall
'what he makes of it'		find the letter: observe his construction of it. For this night, to bed, and dream on the event. Farewell. [*Exit*]
<u>Penthesilea</u>: a warrior queen.	TOBY:	Good night, Penthesilea.
	ANDREW:	Before me, she's a good wench.
<u>beagle</u>: small hunting dog	TOBY:	She's a beagle, true-bred, and one that adores me: what of that?
	ANDREW:	I was adored once too.
	TOBY:	Let's to bed, knight. Thou hadst need send for more money.

8

Writing in character

You may be asked to imagine that you **are** a character, and to write about your thoughts and feelings. If so, ask yourself these questions, in character:

- What do I want? (Love, sex, money, power, a good reputation, revenge … ?)
- What do I fear (Losing a lover, death, hell, being laughed at … ?)
- Who do I like, dislike, love, hate?

You could use a Mind Map to answer the questions.

You may be asked just to write about your character's thoughts and feelings at a particular point in the play, or to write a letter, or perhaps an interview.

A BOX OF TRICKS

Here are two things you should know about **speeches** in Shakespeare plays:

- You may think talking to yourself is a sign of madness, but Shakespeare's characters do it a lot – whether they're mad or not! It's really thinking aloud, and it's called a **soliloquy**.

- It is understood that a character can think aloud and be heard by the audience but not by anyone else on stage. This is an **aside**.

Aguecheek is chicken!

In this passage from *Twelfth Night* we find out more about the characters of Sir Toby Belch and Sir Andrew Aguecheek. Sir Toby is now playing a trick on Sir Andrew. Sir Toby has set up a duel between Viola (a young woman disguised as a man) and Sir Andrew. Sir Toby makes each of his victims terrified of the other.

TOBY:	Why, man, he's a very devil, I have not seen such a firago. I had a pass with him, rapier, scabbard, and all: and he gives me the stuck in with such a mortal motion that it is inevitable; and on the answer, he pays you as surely as your feet hits the ground they step on. They say he has been fencer to the Sophy.
ANDREW:	Pox on it, I'll not meddle with him.
TOBY:	Ay, but he will not now be pacified: Fabian can scarce hold him yonder.
ANDREW:	Plague on it, and I thought he had been valiant, and so cunning in fence, I'd have seen him damned ere I'd have challenged him. Let him let the matter slip, and I'll give him my horse, grey Capilet.

firago: fierce warrior

the stuck in: a fencing thrust

Sophy: Shah of Persia

Speak in character

Try 'hot-seating' with a partner: you're a Shakespeare character who's just stepped out of the play. Your partner is the interviewer. Key questions for Sir Andrew might be: How worried are you about the duel? How much do you care what people think of you? What would you most like to happen at this point?

In the passage below, underline (a) phrases showing that Toby knows about fighting, and (b) phrases that Sir Andrew might not use in polite company.

Read Agony Uncle Brian's reply to an anguished Sir Andrew. Then write Sir Andrew's letter.

Dear Andrew,
  You seem to think that if only you could get Olivia to marry you, everything would be fine. But, reading between the lines, I wonder if she could ever see you as a future husband.
  You say you're a knight with 3,000 ducats a year, and that you're keen on French and music. That's all very well – if she shares your interests. But it sounds as if you spend most of your time getting drunk and clowning about with your friends. Olivia's more likely to love a man who does something useful. And she'll respect you more if you show her you don't <u>need</u> her country house and large fortune.
  As for you 'best mate' Toby, I'm afraid he could be taking you for a ride. Can you trust him? Even if he means well, is he a good influence?
  I'm sure you'll sort yourself out if you drink less and make new friends. Maybe Olivia's not right for you. In any case, if you were adored once, I'm sure it will happen for you again!
  Brian

section round-up

By now you should know:
- how to write **about** character and **in** character
- the four ways in which we learn about Shakespeare's characters
- the importance of their hopes, fears, likes and dislikes.

 Take a break before conjuring up Shakespeare's word magic.

Style and language

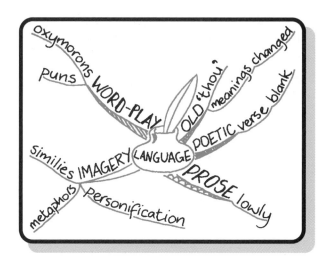

about this section

This section is about Shakespeare's use of words. It will teach you:

- The differences between Shakespeare and modern English.

- About his use of prose and poetry.

- About Shakespeare's imagery and word-play.

Starting to read Shakespeare

When you first read Shakespeare, you may find his 400-year-old English a bit off-putting at times. But the reason it has lasted so long is that – when you get used to it – it's so good. Remember, too, that Shakespeare wasn't a professor: his job was to entertain people – rich and poor, educated and uneducated alike.

You will find some old words, such as *thou* and *thy* for 'you' and 'your'. You will also find some words that are no longer in use, and others that have changed their meaning. One example is *natural*. A football club manager today might say, approvingly, 'The boy's a natural.' To Shakespeare this would mean 'He's an idiot.'

Poetry and prose

Shakespeare's lowly characters, such as Sir Toby (see previous section), speak in **prose** – ordinary sentences with no special line length, and no rhyming. This paragraph is prose. Noble characters usually speak in **verse** – a form of poetry, with lines of a regular length. Sometimes it rhymes, but more often it doesn't.

Shakespeare normally uses **blank verse** – which doesn't rhyme. A typical line of blank verse contains five pairs of **syllables** – a syllable being the smallest pronounceable part of a word when you say it. The word *Shake-speare* has two syllables. ✪ How many syllables does your surname have?

When the line is spoken, the second syllable of each pair has more weight – like someone walking unevenly. Read the following lines out, walking in time:

> *Sleep dwell upon thine eyes, peace in thy breast*
> *Would I were sleep and peace so sweet to rest.*

The syllable pairs are marked in the first line. Mark them yourself in the second. ✪ Which word in the first line has two syllables? How many syllables are there in the second line? How many words?

Imagery

An **image** is a picture. **Imagery** means the kind of word pictures a writer uses to make the writing spring to life. Like most other poets, Shakespeare uses images a lot.

The lines below and the two lines opposite are from *Romeo and Juliet*. The lines on the right are spoken by Romeo to Juliet just before dawn. The lines below Romeo's are spoken by Friar Lawrence, also at dawn.

✪ What pictures do the words paint for you?

Here are three types of image to look for in the lines above, and in any Shakespeare play:

- **Personification** – speaking of a thing as if it were a person.
- **Similes** – comparing one thing with another; often containing 'like' or 'as'.
- **Metaphors** – speaking of a thing as if it were something else that is partly similar (clue to metaphor above – look for something like a chessboard).

One special kind of metaphor used in *Romeo and Juliet* is the strangely named **oxymoron**. This contains two opposite ideas. Someone who uses them may be confused. This is true of Juliet when she hears that Romeo, her lover, has killed her cousin Tybalt (Act 3, scene 2). She feels now that Romeo is not what he seemed.

✪ How many oxymorons can you find?

> *The grey-eyed morn smiles on the frowning night,*
> *Chequering the eastern clouds with streaks of light;*
> *And darkness flecked like a drunkard reels*
> *From forth day's pathway, made by Titan's wheels.**

*Probably the Dawn Goddess's chariot making a path for the sun.

> *O serpent heart, hid with a flowering face.*
> *Did ever dragon keep so fair a cave?*
> *Beautiful tyrant, fiend angelical,*
> *Dove-feathered raven, wolvish-ravening lamb!*
> *Despised substance of divinest show!*
> *Just opposite to what thou justly seems'st!*
> *A damned saint, an honourable villain!*
> *O nature what hadst thou to do in hell*
> *When thou didst bower the spirit of a fiend*
> *In mortal paradise of such sweet flesh?*
> *Was ever book containing such vile matter*
> *So fairly bound? O, that deceit should dwell*
> *In such a gorgeous palace.*

(*bower*: hide)

Word-play

The oxymorons above are not meant to be funny, but they are a kind of word-play. The most common kind of word-play is still popular today. It is the **pun** – based on a double meaning. In *Romeo and Juliet*, one example is when Mercutio knows he is about to die. He still won't be serious (grave) even though he will soon be buried (in a grave):

> *Ask for me tomorrow and you shall find me a grave man.*

105

8

Shakedown

? Copy the style and language Mind Map from the start of this section and add to it the key information that you now know.

? Re-read Juliet's speech with all the oxymorons. In the margins, or on paper, write down key words for the opposites it contains. Draw at least one of the images.

? Try to write four lines of blank verse. They can be about anything you like. Remember, a sentence can carry over from one line to the next, or finish mid-line.

? Invent oxymorons based on opposites of (a) size, (b) beauty, (c) age, (d) speed.

? The word *lie* has two meanings. What are they? Shakespeare uses them to pun. Think of three more words with double meanings (they must sound the same, even if spelled differently). Use a dictionary if you get stuck. Make up puns using these three words.

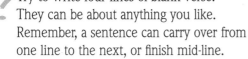

? Read some Shakespeare verse aloud to yourself. Notice the way it sounds, especially the rhythm. Using your finger to tap out the rhythm, try to speak in blank verse yourself. If working with a friend, try a blank-verse conversation.

WORD WIZARD

Shakespeare was a word wizard. He invented words and phrases and popularised new words. *Assassination* is one of his. And if you are ever *in a pickle* through having *too much of a good thing* and need to find *a tower of strength*, you can thank Shakespeare for these phrases. He used about 30,000 different words. A well-educated modern person probably uses only about 15,000.

section round-up

This section has told you about Shakespeare's use of prose and blank verse, and several kinds of imagery. It has also filled you in on his word-play, including puns and oxymorons.

Take a break: you're due on stage in ten minutes!

Performance

about this section

This section is about stage performances of Shakespeare. It tells you:

• What you would need to think about if you were staging a Shakespeare play, so that you can write about your ideas.

• How to write a review of a Shakespeare performance.

Staging

You may be asked to write about how you would **stage** a play or one scene. This means considering the things the people on this page are talking about. They are staging *Macbeth*. They work together, but the director is the most important person.

TO ME, IT'S ABOUT GOOD AND EVIL. I WANT MACBETH TO BE A GOOD SOLDIER BUT A WEAK MAN-LOYAL AT FIRST, BUT FALLING PREY TO EVIL FORCES. TIMING IS IMPORTANT: WE'LL SPEED UP THE ACTION AS THE PLAY MOVES ON, BUT SLOW DOWN FOR THE BIG SPEECHES SO THE AUDIENCE CAN FOLLOW THEM.

DIRECTOR JENNY

SET DESIGNER - IQBAL

JENNY WANTS TO BRING OUT THE GOOD AND EVIL SO I'M GOING FOR CONTRASTS OF DARK AND LIGHT. I'M USING THE SCAFFOLDING FOR THE CASTLE: IT'S HARD-EDGED - NO FRILLS, LIKE THE PLAY. WE CAN HANG DRAPES ON IT AT FIRST, THEN SCRAPS OF RED CLOTH TO SUGGEST BLOOD.

COSTUME DESIGN - DAVID

I WANT THE COSTUMES TO BE TIMELESS, NOT ELIZABETHAN OR MODERN. WE STILL NEED SWORDS FOR THE BATTLE. LADY MACBETH WEARS RED FOR DANGER.

LIGHTING - LUCY

I'M WORKING WITH IQBAL TO CREATE CONTRASTS. SOME SCENES WILL BE QUITE DARK. WE'LL USE ELECTRIC TORCHES FOR BANQUO'S MURDER - AND A STROBE FOR THE BATTLE.

THERE ARE THESE REALLY EERIE ELECTRONIC SOUNDS WHENEVER THE WITCHES APPEAR.

SOUND AND MUSIC - JUSTIN

ACTOR SUZI - LADY MACBETH

I'M IN CONTROL AT FIRST- BUT PITIABLE IN THE END. IF I CAN FRIGHTEN THE AUDIENCE AND THEN GET THEIR SYMPATHY I'VE SCORED A HIT!

8

Writing a review

To review a performance, think about the same things that the director, actors and production team are talking about on the previous page. Comment on how effective their approach is. Ask yourself:

- Do the characters come to life?
- Are they as you imagine them from reading the play?
- Does the production work as a whole?
- For a film, are the settings meant to be realistic? Do they succeed? Is the camera work (close-ups, etc.) effective?

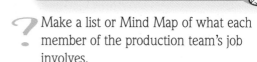

A chance to perform!

 Make a list or Mind Map of what each member of the production team's job involves.

Read the *Macbeth* extract. You are the director. Make notes (on this book if you like), or a Mind Map, to show how you want the actors to speak and act in this scene. Would your ghost be visible to the audience, or only in Macbeth's mind? What does Lady Macbeth do while Macbeth is speaking?

Read the review opposite, then write a review of a Shakespeare play you have seen.

With a friend, act out the scene from *Macbeth*.

What ghost?

The extract below is from *Macbeth*, Act 3, scene 4. Macbeth has had Banquo murdered. Now, at a feast, Banquo's ghost appears to him. No one else sees the ghost. It vanishes and Macbeth pulls himself together. But then ...

[Enter Ghost]

MACBETH: Avaunt! And quit my sight! Let the earth hide thee!
                Thy bones are marrowless, thy blood is cold;
                Thou hast no speculation in those eyes
                Which thou dost glare with.

LADY MACBETH: Think of this, good peers,
                But as a thing of custom: 'tis no other;
                Only it spoils the pleasure of the time.

MACBETH: What man dare, I dare:
                Approach thou like the rugged Russian bear,
                The armed rhinoceros, or the Hyrcan tiger;
                Take any shape but that, and my firm nerves
                Shall never tremble: or be alive again,
                And dare me to the desert with thy sword;
                If trembling I inhabit then, protest me
                The baby of a girl. Hence, horrible shadow!
                Unreal mockery, hence!   *[Ghost vanishes]*

                        Why, so; being gone,
                I am a man again. Pray you, sit still.

REVIEW
George Costigan's *Macbeth*

Every director of *Macbeth* tries to be different. George Costigan's production almost lost track of the play itself. Some lines were added, others cut or moved, especially those of the Witches – who looked very ordinary. At the end, Macbeth is meant to die fighting Macduff, not get shot by Malcolm while dangling on a meat-hook!

None the less, Pete Postlethwaite was convincing as a Macbeth who should have stayed a soldier and couldn't cope with kingship. Patricia Kerrigan was full of energy, but was less persuasive in madness than as an ambitious wife.

One good scene was when Duncan arrives at Macbeth's castle. This production kept him waiting at the gate. His conversation with Macduff was then seen as an embarrassed way of killing time.

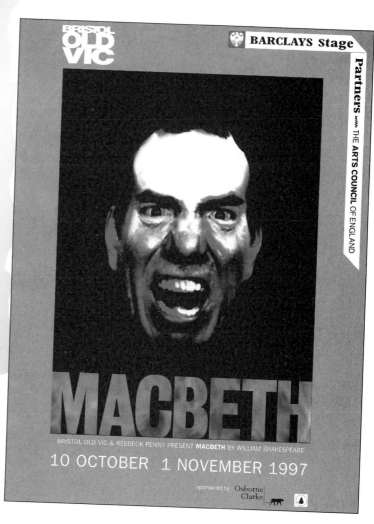

BRISTOL OLD VIC & REBBECK PENNY PRESENT **MACBETH** BY WILLIAM SHAKESPEARE
10 OCTOBER 1 NOVEMBER 1997
sponsored by Osborne Clarke

section round-up

This section has told you:
- About the roles of director, set and costume designers, lighting and sound specialists, and actors in staging a Shakespeare play.
- About how to review a Shakespeare performance.

SPELL-BINDING
To work some memory magic, remind yourself now of what you've learnt. If you've been making a chapter Mind Map, check it against the Mind Map on the next page. Then try the checklist.

8

checklist

Could you now:

	Yes	Not yet

1 Describe the Elizabethan theatre? (pp. 96–7)

2 Name three types of Shakespeare play and say how they differ from each other? (p. 97)

3 Make a Mind Map of one major character in a Shakespeare play?

4 Explain **blank verse**? (p. 104)

5 Name and explain two types of imagery? (p. 105)

6 Say what a play's director does? (p. 107)

If your answer to any of these questions is 'Not yet', look back at the pages shown. If you're still unsure, ask your teacher for help.

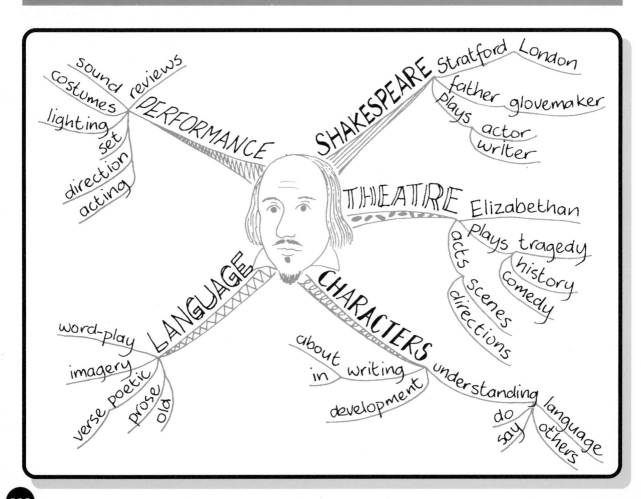

Modern plays

overview

This chapter brings you up to date with drama written after 1900. In many ways, however, modern drama has a lot in common with Shakespeare's plays. Modern audiences enjoy watching plays with strong themes, interesting characters and lively dialogue, just as Shakespeare's audiences did. Work through this chapter to find out about:

- Different types of play.

- Character in drama.

- Writing a playscript.

Types of play

There is one thing all plays have in common: they are written to be performed. The words of a play are meant to be spoken out loud by actors. Actors are told how to say the lines, how to move and how to present their character by the director. Plays can be performed on stage, on television, on film, on the radio. Each type of drama – stage, television, film and radio – has its own particular characteristics.

✪ What are some of the differences and similarities between these types of play? Add your own ideas to the Mind Map at the end of this chapter.

Character

about this section

This section focuses on character. It will help you to understand:

- How character is presented in drama.

- How characters are revealed through dialogue.

- How characters are revealed through their physical appearance.

What's different about character in drama?

Characters in plays are created in the same way as characters in novels and stories. We find out about them through what they look like, what they do and say and what other people think about them.

The big difference is that we find out about characters in plays as we **watch** what is happening and **hear** what is being said; unlike novels and stories, plays don't have passages of description.

The only exception to this is when one character talks about another character. This can reveal a lot about the character being described. It can also tell us something about the speaker, who may of course be expressing his or her own views.

9

Skivers

This extract from a modern play by David Williams
is about what happens when 14-year-old Claire and
Paula have to take part in a race at school.

MISS DUNN:	Right girls. Everybody line up behind the flags, please.
	[Crowded commotion]
	Don't push. Spread yourselves right down the track.
HELEN:	Not fair, miss. The ones at the front get a start on us.
MISS DUNN:	It's four miles, Helen. I'm sure you'll catch up.
CLAIRE:	*[Mimicking]* Not fair, miss.
PAULA:	I don't see why everybody has to run. Why don't they just let the Helen Clarks an' them get on with it. They'll win anyway. We could just stay and cheer.
CLAIRE:	Wouldn't cheer that stuck-up thing.
MISS DUNN:	Claire Morton! What are you doing with your coat on?
CLAIRE:	It's freezing, miss.
MISS DUNN:	Don't be stupid. You can't run in that.
CLAIRE:	Don't want to run.
MISS DUNN:	Take it off.
CLAIRE:	Nowhere to put it.
MISS DUNN:	Give it here. Get into line. You too, Paula Wood. *[Calling]* Everybody ready?
	[Gun fires. A stampede]
CLAIRE:	*[Running]* Hang on, Paula. Don't run so rotten fast.
PAULA:	I'm getting carried away with the rest.
CLAIRE:	We'll be carried off if we keep this pace up. Four miles and we're not out the gate yet.
PAULA:	Helen Clark is.
CLAIRE:	Slow down.
PAULA:	We're last now.
CLAIRE:	Good. That way nobody'll see us skiving off.
PAULA:	How d'you mean?
CLAIRE:	My house is just round the corner. Let's nip in there for a cup of coffee.
PAULA:	We can't do that. We'll be miles behind.
CLAIRE:	They come back the same way, stupid. We'll just tuck in behind them. Nobody'll know.
PAULA:	I don't ....
CLAIRE:	What's the problem?
PAULA:	I don't want people calling me a cheat ....
CLAIRE:	They won't know. Anyway, it's not as if we're trying to win. We're going to be last in any case, so what's the diff .... Come on, if you're that keen on running I'll race you to my house.
	[Claire's kitchen]
CLAIRE:	Want a top-up?
PAULA:	Thanks.
CLAIRE:	There's some chocolate biscuits in that tin.
PAULA:	Shouldn't really but ... go on, then. What sort do you want? Marathon?

What they say and do

What have you discovered about the characters? Choose words and phrases from the list that describe each character and write them in a copy of the chart.

athletic   keen on sport   competitive
unsympathetic   dislikes sport   firm   resentful
reluctant   organiser   sense of humour
comes up with ideas   sense of honour

Miss Dunn	Claire	Paula	Helen

What they look like

What do you think each of the characters should look like on the stage? Think about the kind of physical characteristics and the kind of clothes that will give an idea of what the characters are like. Do they have any particular habits or ways of behaving? Make some notes under each heading in a chart like the one below.

Hint: The characters' appearance should give the audience an immediate impression of what they are like. How can the same games kit be worn in different ways to show different attitudes to sport?

	Miss Dunn	Helen	Claire	Paula
physical appearance				
clothes				
physical habits /mannerisms				

Test it out

After the scene you have just read, Claire and Paula run back to school, to make it look as if they've run the four miles, but they get the timing wrong and arrive first! Here are some lines from the rest of the play. Which line do you think is spoken by which character? Write a name beside each line.

Miss, this isn't fair.

I'd like to know how you two managed to come in ahead of the rest.

We'll be in real bother over this.

What a laugh, eh?

section round-up

If you've worked through this section, you should be clear about how dialogue and physical appearance help to create character in drama.

Have a break before creating your own dialogue!

9

Writing a playscript

about this section

This section reminds you of the main rules for writing drama.

The layout of a script

- **Setting:** Describe the setting at the beginning of the scene, for example (Claire's kitchen)
- **Characters:** Put characters' names on the left-hand side in capital letters, for example CLAIRE
- **Dialogue:** Don't use speech marks, for example CLAIRE: Slow down.
- **Stage directions:** Directions tell the actors what to do and how to say their lines. Put them in brackets, for example CLAIRE: (Running)

Winning words

Remember that in drama most of the information comes through **speech**. We find out about characters' personalities and about the situation through what people say.

Practise it

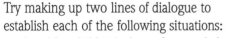

Try making up two lines of dialogue to establish each of the following situations:
- An older child is jealous of a new baby in the family.
- A bank raid.
- Conflict between two students in a lesson.

Artful adapting

Some of the most popular television and film dramas have been adapted from novels; many popular novels have been turned into radio plays. ✪ Which book that you have read would make a good play or film? What main changes would have to be made?

Try this

Write a playscript based on the scenes in the illustration.

Turn this passage into a playscript:

Julie put the cereal packets on the kitchen table and called, 'Get a move on, you lot! I'm going to be late for work if you don't hurry up.'

Harry appeared at the kitchen door. He was still wearing his night clothes. 'I'm really ill, Mum. I can't go to school.'

'Yeah, yeah,' said Julie. 'What is it this time – a chemistry test?' She turned round and looked at him. 'Oh no!' she shrieked. 'What's wrong with your face?'

Write the rest of the scene – or the rest of the script!

section round-up

You've brushed up your scriptwriting skills, and practised writing some scenes.

Take a break before plunging into poetry.

SPELL-BINDING

To work some memory magic, remind yourself now of what you've learnt. If you've been making a chapter Mind Map, check it against the Mind Map below. Then try the checklist.

checklist

Could you now:

	Yes	Not yet
1 Name different types of plays you might read and write? (p. 111)	◯	◯
2 Explain how characters in drama are revealed through what they say? (p. 113)	◯	◯
3 Describe how characters in drama are revealed through their appearance? (p. 113)	◯	◯
4 Set out a playscript? (p. 114)	◯	◯

If your answer to any of the questions is 'Not yet', look back at the pages shown. If you are still unsure, ask your teacher for help.

The Mind Map reminds you of the ideas discussed in this chapter. Copy it and add your own thoughts and examples.

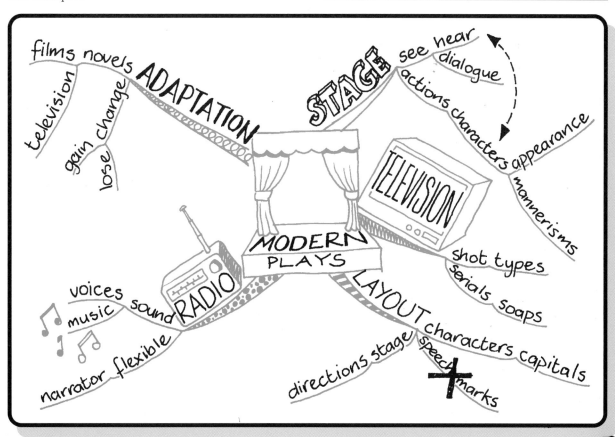

Poetry

overview

This chapter is about how to understand, appreciate and write poetry. It covers:

- Rhythm.
- Word sounds – three types of similarity used in poetry.
- Word pictures – imagery.
- How to write poems.

Ingredients

about this section

This section summarises the most important things that make a poem a poem. They are dealt with fully, using examples, in the rest of the chapter.

Rhythm and metre

A drum rhythm comes from the patterns of timed pauses and light and hard blows. Poetry is similar, but the rhythm is often less regular. Note the rhythm in this limerick by Edward Lear:

> *There was a Young Lady whose eyes*
> *Were unique as to colour and size;*
> *When she opened them wide,*
> *People all turned aside,*
> *And started away in surprise.*

Tap out this rhythm with both hands. Or replace the words with nonsense sounds:

> Be-diddly-diddly *bom* ... (Finish it yourself – aloud!)

A regular rhythm, with a fixed number of **syllables** in each line, is called a **metre**. (A syllable is the smallest pronounceable part of a word. The word 'poet' has two syllables.) To read about Shakespeare's use of metre, see p. 104.

Here are some more limericks by Edward Lear. Try to learn the metre.

> *There was an Old Man with a beard,*
> *Who said, 'It is just as I feared! –*
> *Four Larks and a Wren,*
> *Two Owls and a Hen,*
> *Have all built their nests in my beard!'*

> *There was a Young Lady of Ryde,*
> *Whose shoe-strings were seldom untied;*
> *She purchased some clogs*
> *And some small spotty dogs*
> *And frequently walked about Ryde.*

> *There was an Old Man of the Coast,*
> *Who placidly sat on a post;*
> *But when it was cold,*
> *He relinquished his hold,*
> *And called for some hot buttered toast.*

> *There was an Old Man of the Dee,*
> *Who was sadly annoyed by a flea;*
> *When he said, 'I will scratch it' –*
> *They gave him a hatchet,*
> *Which grieved that Old Man of the Dee.*

Sounds like ...

In the game of Charades, players mime book or film titles. One way is to mime 'Sounds like ...', and then mime a word that sounds like the one you want to suggest – as in the illustration below. Poetry uses three main types of similarity in sound:

- **Rhymes** – as in the illustration and the limerick.
- **Alliteration** – usually when words **begin** with the same sound: *Sly snakes slowly slither.*
- **Assonance** – when words **contain** the same sound: *Turn further, earthling.*

Imagery

Poetry uses **imagery** – word pictures – to make us imagine what something is like. Three important types of imagery are:

- **Metaphors** – describing a thing as if it is something else: 'My bubble of hope ...'
- **Similes** – using 'like' or 'as' to compare: 'His coat flapped in the wind like a crow.'
- **Personification** – describing a thing as if it is a person: 'Night spread her cloak ...'

Quick check

Begin a chapter Mind Map using what you have learnt from this page. Add to it as you read on.

Without looking back, try to write definitions of the following words:
- rhythm
- metre
- syllable
- rhyme
- alliteration
- assonance
- metaphor
- simile
- personification

section round-up

This section has introduced three ingredients of poetry: rhythm, word sounds and imagery.

10

Rhythm

about this section

This section tells you more about how poets use rhythm, giving examples.

Human beings like patterns, and a rhythm is a sound pattern. A restful rhythm can rock a baby to sleep; an exciting rhythm can stir up energy – as in a football chant or dance music.

In good poetry, the rhythm suits the subject of the poem. It also changes slightly to match the poet's ideas as the poem unfolds.

Read the poems in this section aloud. See how the rhythm of each fits the subject and ideas. Listen for:

- galloping horses
- the slow and steady ripening of autumn
- a fast-moving, wind-tossed autumn day
- the quick changes of English weather.
- American Indian drums.

The Highwayman

The wind was a torrent of darkness among the gusty trees.
The moon was a ghostly galleon tossed upon cloudy seas.
The road was a ribbon of moonlight over the purple moor,
And the highwayman came riding –
       Riding – riding –
The highwayman came riding, up to the old inn door.

He'd a French cocked hat on his forehead, a bunch of lace at his chin,
A coat of the claret velvet, and breeches of brown doe-skin.
They fitted with never a wrinkle. His boots were up to the thigh.
And he rode with a jewelled twinkle,
       His pistol butts a-twinkle,
His rapier hilt a-twinkle, under the jewelled sky.

Over the cobbles he clattered and clashed in the dark inn-yard.
He tapped with his whip on the shutters, but all was locked and barred.
He whistled a tune to the window, and who should be waiting there
But Bess, the landlord's daughter,
       The landlord's black-eyed daughter,
Plaiting a dark red love-knot into her long black hair.

And dark in the dark old inn-yard a stable-wicket creaked
Where Tim the ostler listened. His face was white and peaked.
His eyes were hollows of madness, his hair like mouldy hay,
But he loved the landlord's daughter,
       The landlord's red-lipped daughter.
Dumb as a dog he listened, and he heard the robber say –

"One kiss, my bonny sweetheart, I'm after a prize to-night,
But I shall be back with the yellow gold before the morning light;
Yet, if they press me sharply, and harry me through the day,
Then look for me by moonlight,
       Watch for me by moonlight,
I'll come to thee by moonlight, though hell should bar the way."

(Alfred Noyes)

From TO AUTUMN

Seasons of mists and mellow fruitfulness,
　Close bosom-friend of the maturing sun;
Conspiring with him how to load and bless
　With fruit the vines that round the thatch-eaves run;
To bend with apples the moss'd cottage-trees,
　And to fill all fruit with ripeness to the core;
　To swell the gourd, and plump the hazel shells
　With a sweet kernel; to set budding more,
And still more, later flowers for the bees,
Until they think warm days will never cease,
　For summer has o'er-brimm'd their clammy cells.

(John Keats)

AUTUMN

I love the fitful gust that shakes
　The casement all the day,
And from the mossy elm-tree takes
　The faded leaf away,
Twirling it by the window pane
With thousand others down the lane.

I love to see the shaking twig
　Dance till the shut of eve,
The sparrow on the cottage rig,
　Whose chirp would make believe
That spring was just now flirting by
In summer's lap with flowers to lie.

I love to see the cottage smoke
　Curl upwards through the trees,
The pigeons nestled round the cote
　On November days like these;
The cock upon the dunghill crowing,
The mill-sails on the heath a-going.

The feather from the raven's breast
　Falls on the stubble lea,
The acorns near the old crow's nest
　Fall pattering down the tree;
The grunting pigs, that wait for all,
Scramble and hurry where they fall.

(John Clare)

119

A Song for England

An a so de rain a-fall
An a so de snow a-rain
An a so de fog a-fall
An a so de sun a-fail

An a so de seasons mix
An a so de bag-o-tricks
But a so me understan
De misery o de Englishman.

(Andrew Salkey)

Hiawatha

   Down the rivers, o'er the prairies,
Came the warriors of the nations,
Came the Delawares and Mohawks,
Came the Choctaws and Camanches,
Came the Shoshonies and Blackfeet,
Came the Pawnees and Omawhaws,
Came the Mandans and Dacotahs,
Came the Hurons and Ojibways,
All the warriors drawn together
By the signal of the Peace-Pipe,
To the Mountains of the Prairie,
To the great Red Pipe-stone Quarry.

   And they stood there on the meadow,
With their weapons and their war-gear,
Painted like the leaves of Autumn,
Painted like the sky of morning,
Wildly glaring at each other;
In their faces stern defiance,
In their hearts the feuds of ages,
The hereditary hatred,
The ancestral thirst of vengeance.

(Henry Longfellow)

Have you got rhythm?

? The poem 'The Highwayman' has been recorded as a folksong by American singer-guitarist Phil Ochs. What sort of music do you think would fit this poem? Try singing it to a tune of your own, to bring out its rhythm. If you prefer, read it aloud. Beat it out with one hand, exaggerating the rhythm. Emphasise it like this:

The wind *was a* torr*ent of* dark*ness (pause)* among *the* gus*ty* trees.

? Compare how Keats and Clare use rhythm differently to give different views of autumn. Write down or highlight lines that especially seem to match the ideas they contain.

? In the first verse of Clare's poem, 'Autumn', one line starts with four strong syllables instead of two pairs of weak/strong. Which it is? How does this change the rhythm to suggest the movement described. (Answer, p. 128.)

? Copy the lively rhythm of Caribbean poet Andrew Salkey's poem in a poem of your own. You could use repeated phrases as he does ('An a so de ...').

? Write a poem copying the 'drumbeat' rhythm of Hiawatha.

section round-up

By now you should be starting to understand how rhythm is used in poetry: how it fits the subject and mood of a poem, and how it varies to reflect the meaning.

You may need a break now – like the Roman soldier on the next page.

Sounds like ...

about this section

This section is about how poets use similarities in the way words sound. It explains and gives examples of three main types of similarity: **rhyme**, **alliteration** and **assonance**.

Rhyme

Many people think that poems have to rhyme, but they don't. Many poems either have no rhymes at all or use rhymes here and there to match the meaning.

Think of two words that rhyme. Write them down. ✪ Why do they rhyme? The answer lies in how they sound. They begin with different sounds and end in the same sound. For example, *blows* and *nose*. Somehow people like this combination of sameness and difference.

The pattern of rhymes in a poem is called the **rhyme scheme**. In the poem by W. H. Auden, the lines rhyme in pairs. We can label them: AA, BB, etc. This is a very simple rhyme scheme. ✪ How does it suit the soldier speaking the poem, and his mood?

Roman Wall Blues

Over the heather the wet wind blows,
I've lice in my tunic and a cold in my nose.

The rain comes pattering out of the sky,
I'm a Wall soldier, I don't know why.

The mist creeps over the hard grey stone,
My girl's in Tungria; I sleep alone.

Aulus goes hanging around her place,
I don't like his manners, I don't like his face.

Piso's a Christian, he worships a fish;
There'd be no kissing if he had his wish.

She gave me a ring but I diced it away,
I want my girl and I want my pay.

When I'm a veteran with only one eye
I shall do nothing but look at the sky.

(W. H. Auden)

The poem by Maya Angelou starts with the same simple rhyme scheme, as she talks about her hard but boringly repetitive daily work. ✪ How does the use of rhymes change, and why?

WOMAN WORK

I've got the children to tend
The clothes to mend
The floor to mop
The food to shop
Then the chicken to fry
The baby to dry
I got company to feed
The garden to weed
I've got the shirts to press
The tots to dress
The cane to be cut
I gotta clean up this hut
Then see about the sick
And the cotton to pick.

Shine on me, sunshine
Rain on me, rain
Fall softly, dewdrops
And cool my brow again.

Storm, blow me from here
With your fiercest wind
Let me float across the sky
'Til I can rest again.

Fall gently, snowflakes
Cover me with white
Cold icy kisses and
Let me rest tonight

Sun, rain, curving sky
Mountain, oceans, leaf and stone
Star shine, moon glow
You're all that I can call my own.

(Maya Angelou)

10

Alliteration and assonance

Gerard Manley Hopkins was a nineteenth-century poet. His poems are full of the joy of sound. He uses rhyme, both at the ends of lines and in the middle (**internal** rhymes). He also uses **alliteration** (when words or parts of them **begin** with the same sound) and **assonance** (when words **contain** the same sound). Read his poem below aloud. The notes on the left tell you about word sounds; the notes on the right explain difficult words and phrases.

WIZARD FACTS

Gerard Manley Hopkins was a Roman Catholic priest, who lived 1844–89. His poems were first published after his death, in 1918. They are religious, but they also show a delight in nature. A more modern poet who uses words in a similar musical way is Dylan Thomas.

Alliteration: m's

Alliteration (<u>d</u>'s) and internal rhyme (dawn-drawn)

Assonance: <u>ee</u> sounds in 'heel sweeps'

Internal rhyme

Alliteration: 'plód' (accented for emphasis) and 'plough' – connects the two words

THE WINDHOVER:

To Christ our Lord

I CAUGHT this morning morning's minion king-
  dom of daylight's dauphin, dapple-dawn-drawn Falcon, in his
    riding
  Of the rolling level underneath him steady air, and striding
High there, how he rung upon the rein of a wimpling wing
In his ecstasy! then off, off forth on swing,
  As a skate's heel sweeps smooth on a bow-bend: the hurl and
    gliding
  Rebuffed the big wind. My heart in hiding
Stirred for a bird – the achieve of, the mastery of the thing!

Brute beauty and valour and act, oh, air, pride, plume, here
  Buckle! AND the fire that breaks from thee then, a billion
Times told lovelier, more dangerous, O my chevalier!

  No wonder of it: shéer plód makes plough down sillion
Shine, and blue-bleak embers, ah my dear,
  Fall, gall themselves, and gash gold-vermilion.

(Gerard Manley Hopkins)

minion: servant

dauphin: prince

Buckle! the bird's wings fold as it dives down.

chevalier: a knight

sillion: turned earth

gall: injure
vermilion: red

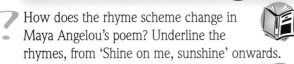

Sounding you out

? How does the rhyme scheme change in Maya Angelou's poem? Underline the rhymes, from 'Shine on me, sunshine' onwards.

? The rhymes in the Auden poem are simple. Try to write different second lines for each pair. Example for first pair: 'I've lice in my tunic and I've got freezing toes.'

? Play some rap music and listen out for internal rhymes.

section round-up

This section has focused on word sounds: rhyme, alliteration and assonance. You should by now be able to explain these, and say how they are used to add to the meaning of a poem.

Imagery

about this section

This section explains how poets use several different types of word picture to make their ideas spring to life in our imagination. (For Shakespeare's imagery, see pp. 104–5.)

Metaphors

A **metaphor** is an image – a word picture – which describes a thing or an idea as if it is something else which is like the thing or idea in some way.

Read the extract from a poem by John Clare, below. Note his metaphors for life, happiness, vain (disappointed) hopes and trouble. The first is 'an hour-glass on the run'.

The R. S. Thomas poem below paints a vivid picture of bright blood, soft as droppings, against the white snow. It contains one metaphor.
○ Where is it?

What is Life?

AND what is life? an hour-glass on the run
A mist retreating from the morning sun
  A busy bustling still repeated dream
Its length? A moment's pause, a moment's
    thought
  And happiness? A bubble on the stream
That in the act of siezing shrinks to nought

Vain hopes – what are they? Puffing gales of
    morn
That of its charms divests the dewy lawn
  And robs each flowret of its gem and dies
A cobweb hiding disappointments thorn
  Which stings more keenly thro' the thin
    disguise

And thou, O trouble? Nothing can suppose,
And sure the power of Wisdom only knows,
  What need requireth thee.
So free and lib'ral as thy bounty flows,
  Some necessary cause must surely be.

(John Clare)

January

The fox drags its wounded belly
Over the snow, the crimson seeds
Of blood burst with a mild explosion.
Soft as excrement, bold as roses.

Over the snow that feels no pity,
Whose white hands can give no healing,
The fox drags its wounded belly.

Personification

Another kind of image, **personification**, describes a thing or an idea as if it was a person. John Clare uses it when he writes about trouble. Modern poets do not use it so often, but the modern Welsh poet R. S. Thomas uses it when he describes the snow in the poem above.

10

Similes

A **simile** highlights what is **similar** between two things. It usually contains the words 'like' or 'as'. Similes are often used in everyday speech. For example, you might say that someone 'smokes like a chimney'. Poets try to use more unusual similes.

Ted Hughes is the Poet Laureate, which means that some people think he is the best living poet in Britain. His poem below is made up almost entirely of similes. ✪ Decide which similes work best. What other similes could he have used? For example, would 'Like a tight oven door' be just as good for the second line?

The Warm and the Cold

Freezing dusk is closing
  Like a slow trap of steel
On trees and roads and hills and all
  That can no longer feel.
    But the carp is in its depth
    Like a planet in its heaven.
    And the badger in its bedding
    Like a loaf in the oven.
    And the butterfly in its mummy
    Like a viol in its case.
    And the owl in its feathers
    Like a doll in its lace.

Freezing dusk has tightened
  Like a nut screwed tight
On the starry aeroplane
  Of the soaring night.
    But the trout is in its hole
    Like a chuckle in a sleeper.
    The hare strays down the highway
    Like a root going deeper.
    The snail is dry in the outhouse
    Like a seed in a sunflower.
    The owl is pale on the gatepost
    Like a clock on its tower.

Moonlight freezes the shaggy world
  Like a mammoth of ice –
The past and the future
  Are the jaws of a steel vice.
    But the cod is in the tide-rip
    Like a key in a purse.
    The deer are on the bare-blown hill
    Like smiles on a nurse.
    The flies are behind the plaster
    Like the lost score of a jig.
    Sparrows are in the ivy-clump
    Like money in a pig.

Such a frost
  The flimsy moon
    Has lost her wits.

    A star falls.

The sweating farmers
  Turn in their sleep
    Like oxen on spits.

(Ted Hughes)

Note
A 'viol' is a musical instrument like a violin. The 'score of a jig' means the written music to a dance tune: the black notes are like squashed flies!

The extract below uses fewer similes than Ted Hughes' poem on the previous page. The poem below describes the poet stepping into the morning 'like a First Communicant'. This means like someone going to take Christian Holy Communion (taking bread and wine as symbols of the body and blood of Christ) for the first time.

❂ How do you imagine a First Communicant would feel? What sort of mood, then, is the poet in?

The Bicycle Ride

I step into the Autumn morning
like a First Communicant
and ride off down the lane,
singing.
Across the frosty fields
someone is mending fences
knock knock knock,
and a twig that's caught
in my bicycle spokes
tinkles like a musical box.
The village smells of wood-ash
and warm horses.
Shining crows rise
into the sky like hymns.

(Selima Hill)

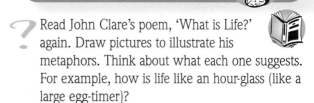

Now you try

❓ Read John Clare's poem, 'What is Life?' again. Draw pictures to illustrate his metaphors. Think about what each one suggests. For example, how is life like an hour-glass (like a large egg-timer)?

❓ In the R. S. Thomas poem, 'bold as roses' is a special kind of simile – a comparison. It is saying that the drops of blood are not just *like* roses, but *as bold as* roses. Why is this a better comparison than, for example, 'bold as brass'?

❓ Read the Ted Hughes poem again. Try to replace at least three of his similes with your own.

❓ The first simile in Selima Hill's poem is 'like a First Communicant'. What are the other two?

❓ How does Selima Hill's poem appeal to our senses, especially hearing and smell?

❓ Start a list of similes and comparisons that you hear in everyday speech, such as 'as quiet as a mouse'. For each, make up at least one more unusual simile of your own.

section round-up

This section has told you more about the use of imagery – word pictures. You should now know something about metaphors, personification and similes, and be able to spot examples in poems and explain why they are used.

 Take a break – before your attention wanders like smoke in a breeze!

10

In your own write

about this section

This section explains how you can put what you've learnt so far into practice in your own poems. It looks at writing in character, at rhythm, rhyme and imagery, and at concrete poems.

What, me?

By now you will understand that there is more to poetry than rhyming – though rhyming can be very effective. From the example poems you should also have got the idea that poems don't always have to be about your own feelings – although many good poems are about the thoughts and feelings that a poet has when looking at the world.

One exciting way to write a poem is to write it **in character**. This means you imagine yourself to be a certain person – a tramp, a soldier, a thief, a princess – and write as if you were that person. You can even imagine you are an animal, a plant or a stream.

If you are writing as a person, you will need to make your language fit the way in which that person might speak. For example, W. H. Auden's poem, 'Roman Wall Blues' is in the kind of straightforward language that a soldier might use. You can see this, too, in the poem by Thomas Hardy, opposite, written in 1902. For example, it uses *nipperkin* for a beer mug.

The Man He Killed

'Had he and I but met
By some old ancient inn,
We should have sat us down to wet
Right many a nipperkin!

'But ranged as infantry,
And staring face to face,
I shot at him as he at me,
And killed him in his place.

'I shot him dead because –
Because he was my foe,
Just so: my foe of course he was;
That's clear enough; although

'He thought he'd list, perhaps,
Off-hand like – just as I –
Was out of work – had sold his traps –
No other reason why.

'Yes; quaint and curious war is!
You shoot a fellow down
You'd treat if met where any bar is,
Or help to half-a-crown.'

(Thomas Hardy)

(*list*: join the army)

WIZARD TIP

When you write a poem, don't expect to wave your magic wand and get it right first time. Be prepared to change words and phrases and redraft it. For example, you might think of a better simile, or realise that one line sounds awkward. Give yourself plenty of space for changes.

Rhyme and rhythm

Should you rhyme and stick to a set metre, as Alfred Noyes does in the ballad of 'The Highwayman' at the start of this chapter? Or should you be free and easy like Selima Hill in 'The Bicycle Ride'? It's up to you, unless your teacher has asked you to try rhyme and metre.

If you use a rhyme scheme, don't let it force you into writing something that makes little sense, or sounds clumsy, just for the sake of the rhyme. If you use a rhyme scheme, you will probably need to use a metre as well. If you use no rhyme scheme or metre, you still need to pay close attention to rhythm and imagery. You can use verses – which are like paragraphs – or not.

Concrete poetry

Your teacher may sometimes ask you to write 'concrete' or 'shaped' poems. This means writing a poem in the shape of the thing you're writing about. The best concrete poems make the shape reflect the meaning of the poem, as does the one below, by Anson Gonzalez.

Little Rosebud Girl
soon to bloom
in splendour
then
to wither
and
f
a
d
e

Have a go time

The real test of this section is in writing poems of your own. However, there are some warm-up exercises and ideas for poems that you can try:

- Write a poem as if you are: a supermarket checkout person, a famous footballer thinking of leaving the game; or a family pet. First, think about what thoughts and feelings this person or animal might have. Use a Mind Map to brainstorm your ideas.

- Think of metaphors or similes for: night falling at the end of a summer evening; tossing and turning unable to sleep; thoughts coming and going in your head; a bed. Jot down or Mind Map your ideas. Then write a poem using some of them.

- Try to write a concrete poem. Some ideas: words and phrases pouring out of an energy-drink bottle; a spinning catherine wheel; a face. You could use colours, and different styles and sizes of print.

section round-up

This section has told you about:
- **Writing poems in character.**
- **Using rhyme and rhythm.**
- **Concrete poems.**

SPELL-BINDING

To work some memory magic, remind yourself now of what you've learnt. If you've been making a chapter Mind Map, check it against the Mind Map on this page. Then try the checklist.

Answers

Answer to question on p. 120
Line 5 – 'Twirling it by the window pane'.
This forces a reader to speed up slightly and 'twirl' the rhythm, suggesting the action of the leaf in the wind.

checklist

Could you now:

	Yes	Not yet
1 Name the main 'ingredients' of poetry? (p. 116)	○	○
2 Explain **metre** and how the rhythm of a poem can match its meaning? (pp. 116, 118)	○	○
3 Give examples of **rhyme**, **alliteration** and **assonance**. (pp. 121–2)	○	○
4 Find examples of metaphors, personification and similes in poems? (pp. 123–4)	○	○
5 Write a poem in character and a concrete poem? (pp. 126–7)	○	○

If your answer to any of these questions is 'Not yet', look back at the pages shown. If you're still unsure, ask your teacher for help.

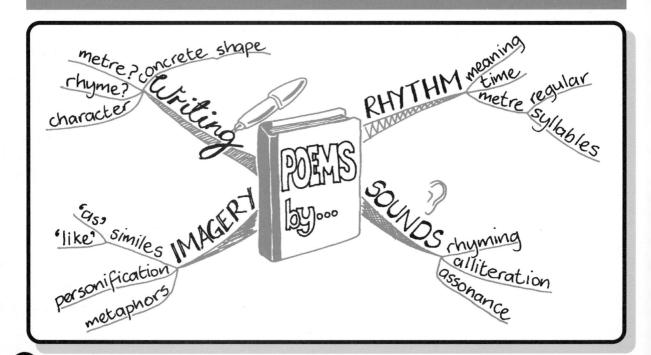

Nuts and bolts of English

overview

This chapter deals with the 'mechanics' of English – the technical aspects that are essential to good writing. Use the chapter to help you to improve your accuracy in spelling, punctuation and grammar. You will also learn the importance of drafting and of checking your work carefully before presenting a final version.

Spelling

about this section

This section gives you some advice about correct spelling. It will help you to become a more confident speller by looking at:

- Words that can be grouped together.

- Some helpful rules.

- Words that are sometimes confused.

Word families

English spelling can be very confusing. For example, you have probably noticed that the same letters or groups of letters are often pronounced differently in different words. ✪ Try reading this sentence aloud quickly:

I ought to be tough and plough on now that my cough has gone, the drought thoroughly is over and I have bought enough.

✪ What other words can you think of that end in *ough*?

You will find it helpful to group together words which have the same letter combinations. These words all contain *ll*:

> *bullet   jewellery   umbrella   marvellous*
> *collapse   parallel*

✪ How can you remember these spellings? You could put them in a sentence like the one made up of *ough* words, or make a series of mental pictures linking the words.

These memory aids are called **mnemonics** (a Greek word – don't pronounce the first *m*). Make up your own mnemonics to help you to remember spellings and spelling rules.

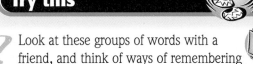
Try this

❓ Look at these groups of words with a friend, and think of ways of remembering them.

- *ent* words
  independent   transparent
  experiment   confident   treatment
- *ful* words
  careful   handful   truthful   wonderful
  restful
- *gu* words
  guidance   guarantee   guitar   guilt
  guardian
- *pp* words
  opportunity   opponent   opposite
  disappoint   happiness

11

Helpful rules

There are rules to help you to remember the right order of letters, and to help you when a word gains or loses a letter when its form changes. Be careful though – there are also exceptions to the rules!

There is a helpful mnemonic for the rule about the order of *i* and *e* in words:

i before e

except after c

when the sound is ee

This reminds you that the usual order is *ie*:
field   niece   believe

but when the letters come after *c*, the order is *ei*:
deceive   receive   ceiling

✪ Read these words out loud:
weird   beige   height   leisure

What do you notice about their sound? The rule only applies when the sound of the word is **ee**.

Here's another useful rule. It's about plurals. Have you ever wondered why the plural of **boy** is formed by just adding an *s*, but the plural of **baby** is **babies**? It's to do with the letter before the final *y*. If there's a vowel (a, e, i, o, u) before the final *y*, just add *s*. If there's a consonant before the final *y* change the *y* to *i* and add *es*.

Apply the rule

What are the plurals of *day   body   city party   key   monkey?*

WIZARD HINTS FOR LEARNING SPELLINGS

Try: look, say, cover, write, check.

Try: finding words within the word; for example, you might travel on a **bus in** to the city to do **business**.

Try: taking a mental photograph of the word.

Try: making up your own mnemonic. Funny ones really work!

Try: tracing the word in the air, on a table, on your friend's back.

Sounds like

Some words sound almost the same, but are spelt differently. Do you feel confident about the difference between:

- there/their/they're
- past/passed
- to/too/two ?

See if you can use each word correctly in a sentence – or get together with a friend and make up a story that uses them.

✪ Try this one: here/hear. Can you think of a way of remembering the difference? (**Hint:** what do you h**ear** with?)

section round-up R

You've learnt some spelling rules and some ways of remembering spellings.

STOP   Have a break before coming to a full stop.

Punctuation

about this section

Punctuation is important because it helps the reader to understand what is being read. It would be very difficult, if not impossible, to make sense of words strung together without any full stops, commas or other punctuation marks. This section will help you to understand how to use:

• Commas and full stops.

• Colons, semi-colons and dashes.

• Apostrophes.

Commas and full stops

Commas

Use commas and full stops very carefully. A common mistake is to use a comma when a full stop should be used. If you remember that you can finish a sentence with a full stop but not with a comma, you won't make this mistake.

Here are three important uses of **commas**.

1 Commas are used to separate parts of a sentence to make the meaning clear. Each of these sentences has the same words in the same order, but in sentence B the addition of two commas makes the meaning entirely different.

A *Adam said his mother was not invited to the party.*

B *Adam, said his mother, was not invited to the party.*

2 Commas are used to separate items in a list:
For the field trip next week you will need to bring a clipboard, a torch, a map and a packed lunch.
Notice that the last two items in a list are usually linked by 'and' instead of a comma.

3 Commas are used to mark off words which are not an essential part of the sentence. You can recognise words like this by the way that they break into the flow of the sentence.
Lisa, however, was invited to the party.
The school canteen, as I told you earlier, is closed for redecoration.

WIZARD TIP

A comma is **never** used to finish a sentence. It is **never** used to join complete sentences. When you come to the end of a sentence, that is, a complete statement, stop and ask yourself how you want to go on. You can use:

• a full stop and a capital letter

• a joining word like 'but' or 'and'

• a semi-colon

• a colon.

Full stops

A full stop marks where a sentence ends. It shows where one statement ends and another one begins. Remember to begin your new statement with a capital letter.

I waited at the bus-stop for half an hour. Finally I decided to walk home.

Test yourself

? Write a sentence using a list of words to describe the items in your school bag.

? Write a sentence using a list of words to describe the actions of a player in a game before scoring a goal.

? Write a sentence giving a list of instructions about how to make your favourite sandwich.

? Write a series of sentences to describe what you do when you get home from school. Use at least three full stops.

Colons, semi-colons and dashes

You can write accurately and fluently without using these punctuation marks, but if you use them properly you will gain marks for style!

Here are two uses of the **colon :**

1 The colon can be used to introduce a list.
 I would like to see the following at lunchtime: Mark, Amy, Justin, Sunil and Maya.

2 The colon can be used to separate two statements when the second statement gives more details of the first.
 Someone must have broken in: the padlock was broken, the door was wide open and the box was gone.

The **semi-colon ;** is used to separate statements. It is stronger than a comma, but not as strong as a full stop. Use it when your two statements are too closely connected to be separated by a full stop and a capital letter.

It was getting late; she looked anxiously out of the window.

✪ Read the Wizard box for more about the semi-colon.

Dashes are used to break a sentence into different parts. They show a more deliberate break than commas, and can be used for emphasis or dramatic effect.

The intruder – whoever he was – left little trace. That's wrong – do it this way.

Practice time

? Use this Mind Map to write a series of sentences. Use a semi-colon where you can.

? Using the colon, write a sentence to say that cold drinks, hot drinks, biscuits and crisps are available from the vending machine.

? Put dashes in this sentence:
 The main problem and I am sick and tired of saying this is the late arrival of the school buses.

Apostrophes

The apostrophe has two important uses that you should know.

1 It shows where letters have been left out in a word.
  I'm going to be late if you don't hurry up. (I'm = I am; don't = do not.)
2 It shows possession.
  My friend's house is quite near. (the house of one friend)
  My friends' parents are all allowing them to go to the concert. (the parents of more than one friend)

WIZ WAYS WITH APOSTROPHES

When you're using the apostrophe to show possession, ask yourself 'Who does this belong to?' Then add either 's or s' depending on how the word ends.

If the word doesn't end with s, add 's: *my friend + 's house*

If the word does end with s, add ': *my friends + ' parents*

WIZARD WARNING!

Don't be tempted to add an apostrophe whenever a word ends with s! Remember – it shows possession or a missing letter.

Test time

 Where should there be apostrophes in these sentences? Add them in the correct places.
(a) Ive got two minutes to get to my friends house.
(b) I dont think that well be late if the buses are on time.
(c) My sisters wont tidy their rooms.
(d)

> **Springs here
> buy your lettuces,
> cucumbers and
> tomatoes.**

section round-up

You should be able to use a range of punctuation marks – commas, full stops, colons, semi-colons, dashes and apostrophes – confidently and accurately.

 Take a break before getting grammatical.

Punctuating conversation

about this section

This section helps you to punctuate conversation accurately. It shows you how to use speech marks and how to set out conversation. It also explains the difference between direct and reported speech.

Speech marks

A good way to raise your grade in English is by writing lively, accurate conversation and dialogue. It is important to punctuate speech correctly, so that the reader can follow the conversation and easily understand which words are spoken by which characters. The rules for punctuating conversation may seem complicated, but with practice they will seem more simple! Here are five rules to help you to punctuate speech.

1   Speech marks are used to show the actual words that are spoken. You can use single speech marks, like this: ' ', or double ones, like this: " ". Just make sure you are consistent.
    "I'd like to see this film," said Will.
    'I'd like to see this film,' said Will.

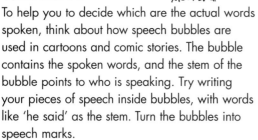

WIZARD TIP

To help you to decide which are the actual words spoken, think about how speech bubbles are used in cartoons and comic stories. The bubble contains the spoken words, and the stem of the bubble points to who is speaking. Try writing your pieces of speech inside bubbles, with words like 'he said' as the stem. Turn the bubbles into speech marks.

2   Each new piece of speech begins with a capital letter.
    'Shall we get tickets for this evening?' Will went on. 'We could ask Chloe to come as well.'
    Luke said, 'Sounds good to me.'

However, you don't use a capital letter at the beginning of a new piece of speech if the sentence is broken up by words like 'he said'.
'I'll meet you outside the cinema,' said Chloe, 'if I can get a lift from someone.'

If you want to check it out, try removing the words 'said Chloe'. Can you see that these words break into the sentence?

3   Each piece of speech must finish with a punctuation mark, which is put **inside** the speech marks. The punctuation mark could be a full stop, a comma, an exclamation mark or a question mark.

Try it out

Finish each of these pieces of speech with a punctuation mark. Write it in.
'What time does the film start ' asked Luke.
'I think it starts at eight o'clock ' said Will.
'That's the best film I've seen for ages ' Chloe exclaimed.
Luke said, 'I don't usually like fantasy movies, but I enjoyed that '

4   If you put words like 'she said' before a piece of speech, put a comma before the speech marks.
    Chloe said, 'What's on next week?'

5   If you put words like 'he said' in the middle of a piece of speech, put a comma or a full stop after them. Use a comma if the sentence continues, and a full stop if you are finishing the sentence and beginning another one.
    'I'll go to the video shop,' said Luke, 'and check if it's in.'
    If you put a full stop, begin the next piece of speech with a capital letter.
    'I'll go to the video shop,' said Luke. 'They might have some new films in.'

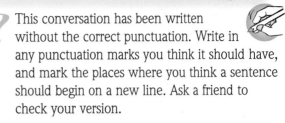

Setting out speech

When you are writing a long conversation, or one between several characters, follow these simple guidelines.

1 Every time there is a new speaker, begin a new line.

   'Three colas, please,' said Chloe.
   'Anything else?' asked the assistant.

2 If there is a long piece of speech spoken by one person, divide it into paragraphs. It is usual to put opening speech marks at the beginning of each paragraph, but closing speech marks only at the end of the final paragraph

   'I can explain why I was late,' said Josh. 'It's quite a long story, but every word is true.' He put down his school bag and drew a deep breath.

   'The first thing was that my alarm clock didn't go off, so I didn't wake up until eight o'clock. I got ready in ten minutes flat and rushed out of the house. I just caught the bus but it broke down.

   'The next disaster was....

Test yourself

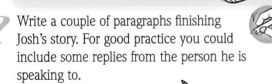

? Write a couple of paragraphs finishing Josh's story. For good practice you could include some replies from the person he is speaking to.

WIZARD TIP

To help you to put new speakers on new lines, imagine that you are a camera filming the conversation for a television or film presentation. Think of a scene from a television drama you watch. When one character is speaking, the camera usually concentrates on that person. When someone else speaks, the camera focuses on them. When you write, take a new line for these different 'camera angles'.

Practice time

? This conversation has been written without the correct punctuation. Write in any punctuation marks you think it should have, and mark the places where you think a sentence should begin on a new line. Ask a friend to check your version.

Is that you Ashley called his mother. Who else do you think it is. Come in here said his mother and don't be so cheeky. Ashley replied I wasn't being cheeky. What's wrong I've had a letter from school said his mother. Oh no said Ashley I didn't think they'd tell you about it

Direct and reported speech

What differences do you see in these two sentences?

A *The drama teacher said, 'I am very pleased with the year's activities. The junior drama group has presented a musical, and the seniors have staged two reviews and a production of Macbeth.'*

B *The drama teacher said that she was very pleased with the year's activities. The junior drama group had presented a musical, and the seniors had staged two reviews and a production of Macbeth.*

In sentence A, the drama teacher's **actual words** are quoted. Sentence B gives the same information, but does it in a different way. Sentence A is an example of **direct speech**. Sentence B is an example of reported, or **indirect speech**.

Check the differences

Decide which is the correct answer and draw a circle around the letter.

 Which version reports the exact words that were spoken?   A   B

Which version gives the meaning but not the exact words?   A   B

Which version uses speech marks?   A   B

As you see, reported speech gives the same information as direct speech, but it is written in a different way. Use this table to help you write reported speech.

Direct speech		Indirect speech
Uses speech marks		Doesn't use speech marks
Gives exact words spoken		Doesn't give exact words spoken
I	becomes	he or she
is or am	becomes	was
have or has	becomes	had
will	becomes	would
liked	becomes	had liked
now	becomes	then
here	becomes	there
this	becomes	that
these	becomes	those
my	becomes	her or his
our	becomes	?
we	becomes	?

Question marks and exclamation marks disappear when you write reported speech!

Direct speech: *Mum asked me, 'Would you like another drink?'*

Reported speech: *Mum asked me if I would like another drink.*

Direct speech: *'I'm not accepting any more excuses!' said the coach.*

Reported speech: *The coach said that he was not accepting any more excuses.*

Can you do this?

Here is an extract from *Great Expectations* by Charles Dickens. A lawyer, Mr Jaggers, visits a young boy called Pip and tells him that his life is going to change. Read what Mr Jaggers says, and then turn his **direct speech** into **reported speech**.

"My name is Jaggers, and I am a lawyer in London. I am pretty well known. I have unusual business to transact with you, and I begin by explaining that it is not of my originating. If my advice had been asked, I should not have been here. What I have to do as the confidential agent of another, I do.

"I am instructed to communicate to you that you will come into a handsome property. It is the desire of the present owner of that property that you be immediately removed from your present sphere of life and be brought up as a gentleman – in a word, as a young fellow of great expectations.

"You are to understand first, Mr Pip, that it is the request of the person from whom I take my instructions, that you always bear the name of Pip. You are to understand secondly, Mr Pip, that the name of the person who is your liberal benefactor remains a profound secret."

section round-up

You should now be able to punctuate direct speech accurately, and be clear about the rules to follow when you write reported speech.

Grammar

about this section

This section helps you to brush up your grammar. When you have finished you should be able to:

- Recognise parts of speech and know how to use them.

- Write accurate and effective sentences.

Why is grammar important?

Grammar is important because it helps us to communicate. We structure our speech and writing by using words in a particular order, following certain rules. You will have learnt most of these rules as soon as you started to speak, and you probably use most of them automatically. For example, you don't say: *went I cinema night last the to.* You just know that the order of words is wrong. We have a range of technical terms to help us to discuss the rules of language.

Parts of speech

Words are divided into **parts of speech** according to the ways in which they are used.

Nouns are words that **name** things.

✪ Match up the pictures with the descriptions of what nouns name.

Nouns name: physical objects you can touch; collections of animals, places or things; feelings and emotions.

Adjectives are words that **describe** nouns (things) more precisely. They answer questions like: what kind of? how many? which?

✪ Underline the adjectives in this sentence:
Put those green apples and these two bananas on the small table, please.

Verbs tell us what is **happening** – they say what someone or something is **doing** or **being**.

✪ Here are some different forms of the same verb. Write a sentence using each one.

sing   sang   had sung   was singing

Adverbs add to the meaning of verbs, describing things that people do more precisely. They usually describe **how** something is done.

✪ Imagine you are at home alone on a dark and stormy evening. You think you hear footsteps outside. Which adverbs from the list would describe the way you behave?

lazily   fearfully   vaguely   nervously   cautiously happily

Conjunctions are words that join sentences together.

✪ Choose three conjunctions from the list to join together these two sentences:
The dog was sick. Jamie went to the disco.

and   but   when   before   so   until   because

✪ How does the meaning of the sentence change when you change the conjunction?

Prepositions are the little words like **in, on, through** that show where things are in relation to each other.

✪ Use different prepositions to complete this sentence as many times as you can:
The cat went ... the fence.

Pronouns are words which take the place of nouns. We use them instead of repeating the name.

● Which pronouns would you use to avoid repetition in:

Lisa and Amy have been friends for ages. Lisa and Amy first met in junior school. Recently Lisa told Amy that Lisa's family was moving house so Lisa and Amy would not be living near each other.

Sentence construction

A sentence is a group of words that is complete in itself. A **simple** sentence has one main piece of information with one main verb.

I caught the bus.
The parrot flew out of the cage.

A series of simple sentences can be boring. You can make your writing more varied and interesting by constructing more complicated sentences. The easiest way is to join sentences together by using conjunctions. (See 'Parts of speech'.) You can also create different types of sentences by using **clauses**. A clause is a group of words that does not make complete sense until it is linked to the main sentence. Look at this example:

When I got up – this is a clause. By itself, it doesn't make complete sense.

Here are two ways of linking this clause to the sentence: *Dawn was breaking.*

Dawn was breaking when I got up.
When I got up dawn was breaking.

Varied sentences

❓ Rewrite these simple sentences in a more interesting style, using different sentence structures.
Romeo and Juliet lived in Verona. They met at a ball. The ball was given by Juliet's father. They fell in love. Their families were enemies.

❓ Write a simple sentence describing each of these pictures. Then tell the story using different sentence structures.

Noun-verb agreements

An important rule of grammar is that there must be agreement between the number of the noun and the form of the verb. If the noun is singular, the verb must be singular as well.

*Lee **was** going to the leisure centre.*
*Lee and Sasha **were** going to the leisure centre.*

Getting the agreement right can be more difficult in a longer sentence.

*Lee and Sasha, who used to go to the same school, **were** going to the leisure centre.*

Some dialects (see page 10) have their own particular use of pronouns and verbs. On the whole, these variations are used in speech rather than in writing.

section round-up

You should now be able to recognise the most important parts of speech, and understand how grammar rules can help you to write accurately.

Drafting

about this section

This section emphasises the importance of writing a first draft and improving it. It focuses on vocabulary and expression.

It is always a good idea to write a first draft of any English assignment. Very few people can produce their best essays or stories at the first attempt. It is helpful to follow this sequence:

1 **Plan** (Make a Mind Map.)
2 **Draft 1** (Write on every other line so that you have plenty of room to make changes.)
3 **Check** (Go over your first draft and improve it.)
4 **Draft 2** (Write out the improved version.)

WIZARD TIP FOR DRAFTING
Try different ways of improving your first draft.

11

Drafting exercise

? Read Jason's draft account of a camping holiday. How can it be improved? Some of the vocabulary and grammar has been changed. Make any other changes to the expression and grammar that you think would give the account more accuracy and more style.

It took us ages to get ready. It poured down as we cycled up the hill. ~~Me and~~ my friends were soaked, we arrived at the site late in the afternoon. Our cloths and shoes ~~and I h~~ were ~~soaked~~. My hair was stuck to my head drops of water ran down my face.   drenched

'Was this a good idea' asked Luke. I didnt answer.   Inden

Then we had to put up the tent. It had stopped raining by then.   ×2

We struggled a bit with the tent although we had practiced putting it up in Lukes back garden. Somehow it wasn't the same in the middle of this soaking wet field with Steve and Luke mesing about and pretending to fall over all the time!

When we were putting the tent up I slipped over on the mud and got hurt. Then two girls arrived at the sight next to us they got their tent up in no time! They looked at us very dissapproving and I don't know about the others but I felt a bit sort of stupid. Then we finally got the tent up. Then we sat down to think what to do next.

'I think we should have something to eat' said Luke 'Your always hungry' said Steve. The girls heard this and laughed. I dont know why it wasn't that funny.

'Theres a shop over there' said one of the girls. 'Were going over in a minute. Do you want to come with us' Steve and Luke nudged each other. Their so immature. 'Could do' said Steve like he didnt care. Then they went to the shop. I walked behind them. This is going to be great, I thought. I should of stayed at home.

section round-up

You've practised drafting and learnt about producing and checking a first draft. Go on to the next section to find out about the next stage in the drafting process.

Proofreading and presentation

about this section
This section takes you through what to do when you have written your second draft. You will learn how to improve your accuracy, and how to present your work effectively.

What is proofreading?

Proofreading is the final checking stage. When you proofread you go through your second draft and check spelling, punctuation and grammar. Use a dictionary to check spelling even if you are using a word processor that has a spellcheck. Your computer will not recognise words that you have confused, such as *rein* and *rain* or *passed* and *past*.

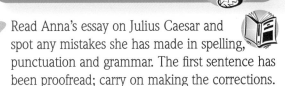

Try this

? Read Anna's essay on Julius Caesar and spot any mistakes she has made in spelling, punctuation and grammar. The first sentence has been proofread; carry on making the corrections.

Shakespeare makes this scene tense by setting it in the ~~middet~~ middle of the night in Brutus's garden. Brutus cant sleep he is in a state of indesicion as thoughts whirl round in his brain. He is going over the reasons why Caesar should die and is convincing himself that his death would be a good thing for rome. The excitment build up as a letter is thrown in his window and is continued as the conspiraters arrive. There faces are hidden in their cloaks so that they won't be recognised.

? Read Sam's description of what it was like leaving his last school. Proofread it carefully and correct any mistakes in spelling, punctuation and grammar.

My last day at middle school was a time of rememberance. As I walked through the gates for the last time I remembered all the good times the arguements with each other and the fun what we had. Me and my friends were in the same group from the beggining and now we would be split up. Me and Jason was the only ones who would be going to this school. I could here the sound of crying and teachers voices being kind their was lots of presents and cards being exchanged.

? Read Hanif's discussion of smoking. Proofread it carefully and correct any mistakes in spelling, punctuation and grammar.

I think smokeing should be banned in public places it is becoming less frequent however. There is now more awareness that smoking can damage your health and other peoples. People accept more that it is anti-social and dangerous in spite of this lots of people particularly young ones still smoke. This is proberbly because they want to look cool. Advertisments and other media images are partly to blame

You will find corrected versions at the end of this chapter. ✪ Did you spot all the mistakes?

Presentation

When your final draft is ready you will want to present it as attractively as possible. If you are word-processing your work there are lots of ways you can make it look good on the page – but do remember that you will get marks for the quality of what you write rather than the clever way you have used space or different typefaces!

Of course, your exam answers will be handwritten. Practise to make your handwriting clear and attractive. Make sure that your letters are even and clearly distinguishable, and that they slant the same way. The overall look of a page will be improved if you leave clear margins all round. If you use headings and subheadings, make them stand out from the rest of the text. If you underline, use a ruler!

Setting out quotations

When you write about the material you have read you will want to quote from it to illustrate and back up your points. Setting out quotations clearly and attractively will add to the effective presentation of your work. Remember that **quotation marks** go around the **actual words** from the text.

If you want to use a **short quotation** it is a good idea to include it in your discussion, like this:
The words, 'Benjamin's face fell even further' and 'he felt more trapped and miserable than ever', give me the impression that Benjamin was not enjoying the surprise flight.

If you want to use a **long quotation** it is a good idea to put it in a block in the centre of the page. You don't need to use quotation marks if you quote like this.
We see that Romeo has a good reputation, and that Lord Capulet wants him to be treated as a guest.

> *And, to say the truth, Verona brags of him*
> *To be a virtuous and well-governed youth:*
> *I would not for the wealth of all the town*
> *Here in my house do him disparagement.*

Titles of books

You should make it clear when you are referring to the title of a book, poem, play, song or film. This is particularly important when you need to make it clear if you are referring to the work as a whole or a character. One way is to put the title in quotation marks. Use capitals for the first word and for keywords.
'Romeo and Juliet'   *'The Highwayman'*
'The Canterbury Tales'

Sometimes you will see titles in *italics*, as in this book, or you might see them <u>underlined</u>. These are accepted ways of making a title stand out, but when you are handwriting your answers, quotation marks are probably the clearest.

Paragraphs

If you plan your answer carefully you will have a note of what material should be in each paragraph. Make sure that your reader can see where every paragraph begins and ends. Begin your paragraphs a little way in from the margin – indented – and try to line them up so that each one starts at the same point on the page. There is no need to indent the first paragraph after a heading. Try not to begin each paragraph with the same word, like '*I*'.

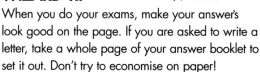

WIZARD TIP
When you do your exams, make your answers look good on the page. If you are asked to write a letter, take a whole page of your answer booklet to set it out. Don't try to economise on paper!

section round-up

You should now have an eagle eye for proofreading, and have some ideas about presenting your work effectively.

Answers

Corrected version of proofreading exercise (p. 141)

Brutus can't sleep; he is in a state of indecision as thoughts whirl round in his brain. He is going over the reasons why Caesar should die and convincing himself that his death would be a good thing for Rome. The excitement builds up as a letter is thrown in his window and is continued as the conspirators arrive. Their faces are hidden in their cloaks so that they won't be recognised.

My last day at middle school was a time of remembrance. As I walked through the gates for the last time I remembered all the good times, the arguments with each other and the fun we had. My friends and I were in the same group from the beginning and now we would be split up. Jason and I were the only ones who would be going to this school. I could hear the sound of some people crying and teachers' voices being kind. There were lots of presents and cards being exchanged.

I think smoking should be banned in public places. It is becoming less frequent, however. There is now more awareness that smoking can damage your health and other people's. People accept more that it is anti-social and dangerous. In spite of this lots of people, particularly young ones, still smoke. This is probably because they want to look cool. Advertisements and other media images are partly to blame.

checklist

Could you now:

Yes   Not yet

1 Spell words with *ei* or *ie*? (p. 130)

2 Remember the rule for making words plural? (p. 130)

3 Describe some ways of learning spellings? (p. 130)

4 Explain the difference between to/too/two? (p. 130)

5 Give three uses of commas? (p. 131)

6 Know when to use a full stop? (p. 131)

7 State two uses of the colon? (p. 132)

8 Explain how to use the semi-colon? (p. 132)

9 Know when to use an apostrophe? (p. 133)

10 Punctuate speech? (p. 134)

11 Describe what a noun is? (p. 135)

12 Explain the difference between adjectives and adverbs? (p. 137)

13 Know when to use a preposition? (p. 137)

14 Explain what a pronoun is? (p. 138)

15 Use a conjunction correctly? (p. 137)

16 Remember how to draft and proofread? (pp. 139–42)

If your answer to any of these questions is 'Not yet', look back at the pages shown. If you're still unsure, ask your teacher for help.

Sitting your SATs

overview

SATs are the tests that you will be given when you are 14. These tests are taken by all 14-year-old students on the same day, and they test what you have learnt during Key Stage 3. This chapter will help you to perform in these tests as well as you can. The chapter reinforces some of the ideas in the introduction to this book so, before going on, turn back to those pages and refresh your memory. At the end of the chapter you will know:

- Good ways to revise.

- How to prepare for the test.

- How to answer the questions.

This Mind Map shows some of the things to think about when you are getting ready for and doing your SATs. Add to it as you work through the chapter.

How to revise

about this section

This section focuses on revision. It will encourage you to find effective ways of learning and remembering what you learn.

First of all

Before you begin revision, you need to know what to revise. Check that you are clear about what will be tested. The examples of papers and timings given in this chapter may change, so check with your teacher to make sure what papers you will be sitting and how long they will be. You will have two papers.

- **Paper 1** lasts 1 hour 30 minutes. In this paper you will be given two pieces of different kinds of writing to **read**. These could be a story, a poem, a newspaper article, a letter, or an advertisement. You will show that you **understand** the pieces of writing by answering questions on each one. Then you will choose a **writing** task based on the passages.

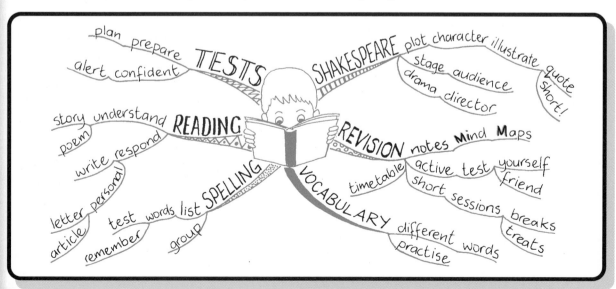

- **Paper 2** lasts 1 hour 15 minutes. In this paper you will write about the **Shakespeare** play you have been studying in class. You will do one task out of a choice of two. The **extract** you have studied will be printed in a booklet given to you with your exam paper.

Check it out

? Have you read different kinds of writing? Have you written in a variety of forms? Tick the list, and add any other examples.

	read	written
story		
poem		.
newspaper article		
letter		
diary		
advertisement		
article		

If there are any gaps, look back through this book for examples of different kinds of writing and for suggestions for your own writing. If you need more help, ask your teacher.

? Finish these sentences:
The name of the Shakespeare play I am studying

is ....

The extract that I am studying is ....

....

Revising for the English paper

Careful revision and preparation will help you to show that you can write confidently in different styles, keep the reader interested and spell and punctuate accurately.

Aim for accuracy

It important that you write as accurately as you can. Try these methods:

? Make a list of words you find difficult. Ask a friend or someone in your family to test you on them.

? Choose some ideas from the Wizard box (p. 130) on ways of learning spellings.

? Do this with a friend. Each of you copy out a paragraph from a newspaper, leaving out all the punctuation marks. Swap copies and write out the paragraph with correct punctuation. Check your version against the original!

Vary your vocabulary

Your writing will be more lively and interesting if you use a range of vocabulary. Try these ideas:

? Choose a word that can be overused – *nice* is a good example. Jot down lots of examples of how you might use the word – a *nice* meal, a *nice* day, etc. For each example, see how many different words you could use instead. (You could do this by yourself, or with a friend or someone at home.)

? When you come across a new word in your reading, follow this process: **1** Write it down **2** Practise saying it out loud **3** Use the word at least once during the day.

12

Revising for the Shakespeare paper

Careful revision of the play you are studying will help you to show detailed knowledge of the chosen extract, and your appreciation of its dramatic qualities.

Task time

Plot

? Make a Mind Map summarising the whole play.

? Tell the story of the play to someone who doesn't know it.

Characters

? Make a Fact File for each of the characters.

Atmosphere

? Decide what music you would choose to accompany different parts of the play.

Language

? Copy out important lines from the play on to cards. Pin up the cards where you will often see them.

? Imagine that your group is going to perform the scene you have been studying. Describe to a friend how you would want the actors to play their parts and how you want the audience to react to the scene.

? Read Chapter 8 of this book for ideas about studying Shakespeare.

WIZARD REVISION TIPS

- Use Mind Maps.

- Form a revision group with one or two friends.

- In your group, test each other and discuss ideas.

- Make a revision timetable.

- Take frequent breaks.

WIZARD WORDBOX

Have you ever thought about where the word *revision* comes from? It is made up from:

re = back or again
vision = sight

So when you *revise* you are taking another look at work you have done, to improve it, or to learn it for tests.

✪ What other words do you know beginning with *re*? Try looking in a dictionary for examples. Now you know what *re* means, try to work out the meaning of unfamiliar words. What about words that contain *vision* or forms that come from *vision* – *vid, vis*?

section round-up

You should now be clear about what you should revise, and how to revise effectively.

Take a break before tackling the tests.

Testing times

about this section

This section deals with the test papers. It gives you some ideas about how to write the best possible answers, and helps you to understand what examiners are looking for.

Exam hints

The tests will give you an opportunity to show what you can do. On the exam day, try to be alert and positive. Be ready to do your best, and look forward to demonstrating the skills you have developed!

Before the tests

Some forethought will help you to be calm and confident on your test day. Look at the illustration.
○ What advice would you give Matt about how to prepare? Write your suggestions in the box.

Have you eaten my best pen?

What do you think?

I was late for breakfast – better get a sugar fix!

During the English test
Reading task

- Read the instructions carefully – your teacher might read them to you. Make sure you understand how many questions to answer from each section. If you are not sure, ask.
- Read each passage twice. Skim read the first time, to get the general sense of it, then read it more slowly.
- Try to write several paragraphs for each answer. Never try to answer in just a single sentence! The questions will probably ask you to look at certain lines in the passage. Even if you think you remember the lines and what they say, look back at them. They will give you ideas for your answer.
- The question may be followed by some suggestions about what you should comment on. Follow these suggestions!
- Proofread your work when you have finished.

Writing task

- Read all the choices – don't just go for the first one! Then read them again.
- Plan your work. You could make a Mind Map and number the branches for the order of your paragraphs.
- Try to make your writing interesting. Look at Chapter 11 for ways to vary your sentence construction.
- Try to use varied vocabulary.
- Take care with spelling and punctuation.
- Use any suggestions given on the test paper about points you could include – they are there to help you do your best work.

Before the exam – some tips

MAGIC TIP TIME

Be a time wizard. With your teacher's help, work out how much time you should spend on each section. Allow time for planning and time for checking. Write your decision here:

English – Paper 1

	Reading	Planning	Writing	Proofreading	Total time
Section A					
Section B					
Section C					
					1 hr 30 mins

English – Paper 2

(Shakespeare)

During the Shakespeare test

- Read each task before you decide which one to do. Then read them again.
- Plan your work. You could make a Mind Map and number the branches for the order of your paragraphs.
- Use any suggestions printed on the test paper.
- Try to use a variety of sentences. Look at Chapter 11 for ways to vary your sentence structure.
- Try to use interesting vocabulary.
- Take care with spelling and punctuation.
- Look at these illustrations of different ways of writing an answer to the Shakespeare question. Put a tick by the good ideas and a cross by the not-so-good ideas.

section round-up

You should now have some good ideas about how to do your best in the test.

Take a break before sampling some questions.

Sample questions and worked examples

about this section

This section will make you familiar with the kind of question you may be asked, and gives you some examples of answers.

English

What will I be given to read?

Be prepared for any kind of passage in your English paper. Here are some examples of the kinds of extracts that have been set:

- a passage from *The Endless Steppe* by Esther Hautzig (Chapter 5 has an extract from this novel)
- a British Red Cross appeal
- a short story by Sylvia Plath
- a newspaper article on bullying
- a passage from *Polar Dream* by Helen Thayer
- an advertisement for a holiday cruise.

The passages will be linked in some way, usually by theme. Other types of passage you could be given

include poems and play extracts. ✪ Think of some more examples of types of writing.

What will I write about the passages?

You will be asked questions designed to test your understanding of and response to the passages. Questions on fiction often focus on characters' thoughts, feelings and relationships. Questions on non-fiction and media often focus on the purpose of the piece of writing and the use of language and other techniques, such as layout, to achieve its aim.

What writing tasks will I be given?

You will be given a choice of topics, which may include stories, letters or newspaper articles. Here are some examples of the tasks that have been set:

- an incident in which you were blamed for something you did not do
- a newspaper article about bullying
- an incident in which you had to leave a place you knew well
- a letter to parents asking for support in fundraising for a charity
- the pros and cons of dangerous sports.

Sample answer

This is part of Sonia's essay on the topic of dangerous sports. The question asked students to include examples of dangerous sports, the reasons why people do them and the problems that can arise, and whether there should be limits to what people are allowed to do.

Dangerous sports appeal to people because they provide a challenge and a thrill. Imagine climbing a cliff face with a sheer drop beneath you and the sea crashing against the rocks, or skydiving through the air with the ground rushing towards you. There must be a great sense of achievment when you get to the top of a mountain or a cliff, or land safely in your balloon.

✓ There can be problems though. If someone doesn't prepare properly and makes mistakes they can end up in a perilous situation and things can go wrong. They may encounter bad weather conditions, or find there equipment isn't adequate.

Spelling slip (sheer)

Good vocabulary

Spelling slip (achievment)

Good examples
Good sentence structure

New paragraph
Good

Spelling slip (there)

12

Shakespeare

What kind of task will I be given?

The tasks you are given will be based on the extract you have studied. You may be asked to write about characters, plot, atmosphere or language. The kinds of questions may involve:

- showing the differences and similarities between characters
- giving your opinion about who is to blame for particular events

- imagining you are a character and writing about your thoughts and feelings
- describing how the audience might react to a character or scene
- showing your understanding of a character's feelings and behaviour.

Sample answer

Here is part of Lee's essay. The task was: *Imagine you are Romeo. Write your thoughts and feelings after the party.*

Knowledge of plot — Good

I was so badly in love with Rosaline that when I found out that she was invited to the party and Benvolio suggested that we should go so that he could prove to me that Rosaline was a crow compared to the dove-like women who would be there, I felt that I just had to go. No matter what Benvolio said, I knew no-one would compare with Rosaline and I longed to see her.

Reference to text — Good

Shows understanding of Romeo's feelings

Knowledge

When we arrived, we tried to blend in. There would be real trouble if we were discovered at our enemy's house! Then I saw her, the most beautiful creature that I have ever seen, the gentlest looking girl that your eyes ever saw. She glowed like a jewel.

Conveys feeling of drama

Reference to text

Preparing and planning

You may be tempted to start writing straight away – but don't! The time you are given for each paper includes planning time. If you use this time effectively you will stand a much better chance of doing your best work.

The first thing to do is to **read the questions carefully**. In both your Shakespeare paper and your English paper you have a choice of questions.
✪ How do you decide which one to do?

Be choosy

Here are two steps to help you to choose.

1 Read the description of each task twice. Ask yourself if you understand what you are being asked to do.
2 Underline the keywords in the description of the task. The keywords are the ones that tell you what you should focus on in your answer.

Look at these three examples of different types of question.

1 **How do you think the audience's impression of Caesar might change and develop as they watch this scene?**

The keywords in this question are: **audience's impression, change and develop**.

The question is asking you to discuss how the audience's opinion of Caesar changes through the course of the scene. To answer this, you will consider the way Caesar is portrayed at the beginning of the scene, and present your ideas about how what happens in the rest of the scene might change, or strengthen, an audience's opinion.

2 **What are the similarities and differences between Mercutio and Tybalt and who do you think is most to blame for their deaths?**

The keywords in this question are: **similarities, differences, who do you think** and **blame**.

The question is asking you to discuss how like and unlike each other the characters are, and to give your opinion about their deaths.

3 **Imagine you are Juliet. Write your thoughts and feelings explaining why you have to take this desperate action.**

The keywords in this question are: **imagine you are, thoughts, feelings** and **explaining**. The question is asking you to write as if you are Juliet and to express your feelings about the situation you are in.

Knowing what the question requires helps you to make a good choice. You may like the kind of question that asks you to discuss how an audience sees a character; your friend might enjoy pretending to be a character and expressing emotion in a more personal way. Go for the task that offers you the opportunity to show your knowledge and understanding of the play in the kind of answer you enjoy writing.

Try it out

 Now apply the same steps to the English paper. Here are the tasks you have to choose from.

Write about how you think old people should be treated by their family and in the community.
or
Write about someone who has an experience of being isolated and cut off from other people.

Hint: You should have noticed that the first task requires you to give your ideas on a topic, while the second task gives you the opportunity to write imaginatively.

 Here are some of the phrases used to introduce tasks. For each one, practise writing a sentence or part of a sentence as an answer.

What do you learn from the passage	I learn from the scene/passage that
How do you know	
Why do you think	
Describe	
Explain how	
In what ways	
How does the poem/ story suggest	One way the poem/ story suggests … is

Planning time

When you have decided which question to answer, spend some time planning what you will write. You should jot down the main ideas you want to cover, group them under headings, and decide the order in which you will present them.

12

WIZARD TIP

Every question on your test papers gives you advice and suggestions about what to include in your answer. It's a very good idea to use these suggestions!

Craig chose to do the following writing task:

Describe a person you know who has influenced you or been very important in your life.

The suggestions given included:
- you could describe what you and other people see in the person you have chosen;
- you could include some memories which show what the person is like.

These are the planning notes that Craig made to help him to organise his answer.

> *Who? – my dad*
>
> *Why important? – has taught me important lessons, has set good example*
>
> *What I see in him: – courage (illness), always joking, listens*
>
> *What other people see in him – good friend, works for charity, generous*
>
> *Memories – making a joke when Lauren burnt his dinner, listening to my side of fight at school*
>
> *Beginning? – description of appearance? – something to show what he's like*
>
> *Ending? – the future? refer back to beginning?*

Writing it up

Here's how Craig began his piece of writing.

> *A vivid picture I have of my father is of his short sturdy figure leaning forward to listen to what I am saying. His forehead is creased as he concentrates, and he runs his fingers through his wiry hair. My father has been a great influence in my life. He has taught me important lessons about how to treat other people, and has given me a good example to follow.*

The time Craig spent planning his answer was well worth it. Notice that he thought about an effective beginning and jotted down specific examples to use as illustrations. He followed closely the given suggestions and based his planning around them.

Supertips for test answers

- Read the passages carefully.
- Read the passages more than once.
- Use a coloured pencil to underline important or striking words and phrases.
- Always refer back to the passage, even if you think you can remember what it said.
- Always write in sentences.
- Always write in paragraphs.
- Notice the number of marks given to each question and make sure you write enough.
- Use a variety of words.
- Use a variety of sentence structures.
- Leave time for checking.
- Enjoy yourself!

section round-up

You should now know the kind of question you will be asked, and you should understand the kind of evidence of your ability that an examiner will look for.

SPELL-BINDING

To work some memory magic, remind yourself of what you've learnt. If you've been adding to a chapter Mind Map, review it now. Then try the checklist.

checklist

Are you clear about:

	Yes	Not yet
1 The kinds of questions you will answer in your tests? (pp. 144–5, 149–50)	○	○
2 How to revise spelling? (p. 145)	○	○
3 How to revise punctuation? (p. 145)	○	○
4 How to revise vocabulary? (p. 145)	○	○
5 How to revise Shakespeare? (p. 146)	○	○
6 How to go about answering the questions? (p. 147)	○	○

If your answer to any of these questions is 'Not yet', look back at the pages shown. If you are still unsure, ask your teacher for help.

Self-checker

Use this page to help you decide what 'nuts and bolts' of English you need to work on. Look at ten pages of work your English teacher has marked. Make a mark under 'How often', below, every time you find a particular type of mistake. Then add them up. Repeat the exercise once a month to check your improvement.

Mistakes made	How often	Total
Not using capitals for 'I', names or new sentences		
Using commas where there should be a new sentence (see p. 131)		
Apostrophes of ownership in wrong place (e.g. cat's singular/ cats' plural) (see p. 133)		
Confusing accept (I accept the blame) and except (everyone except me)		
Confusing of/off/'ve (the tin of sweets must've fallen off the lorry)		
Confusing their/there/they're (they're leaving their cat over there)		
Confusing we're (we are), where (place), wear (clothes).		
Misspelling words ending in ible/able/uble (e.g. possible/impassable)		
Single/double letter spellings (e.g. possess, sloppy)		
Plurals misspelt (e.g. potatoes, pennies)		
Other spellings		
Awkward word order		

Glossary

If a word in the explanation is printed in **bold**, this means that it has its own entry.

accent the way people speak. This includes two things: (1) pronunciation of individual words; (2) intonation – the musical rise and fall of the voice. Accent depends on where people come from and on their social background.

Act a division of a play, rather like a chapter in a book.

adjectives describing words, telling us more about a **noun** or **pronoun** (e.g. The house was *spooky*; it was *huge*.).

adverbs words which tell us more about **verbs** or **adjectives** (e.g. She spoke *loudly*; the bath was *beautifully* clean.).

alliteration repetition of a sound at the beginnings of words (e.g. *burn*, *bubble*).

aside a short speech spoken by one character in a play, as if thinking aloud, not meant to be heard by others on stage.

assonance repetition of vowel sounds (e.g. The h*i*gh d*i*ver tr*ie*d the *i*cy water.).

audience the people watching a play or a television programme, or reading a book; also the people at whom an advertisement is aimed.

autobiography someone's life story written by that person.

bias supporting one side, or one **opinion**, more than another. Writing can be deliberately or accidentally biased.

biography someone's life story written by someone else.

blank verse the kind of non-rhyming verse, with five pairs of **syllables** to each line, in which Shakespeare usually writes.

cliché an overused phrase (e.g. City were *over the moon* at winning the cup.).

closed question a question that invites a yes/no answer (e.g. Were you upset?) See also **open question**.

colloquial ordinary, everyday (speech). 'Fancy a bite to eat?' is colloquial. 'Would you like something to eat?' is not.

comedies humorous plays; Shakespearean comedies also have a lot of word-play, confusion and disguise, and usually end with marriages. *Twelfth Night* is a comedy.

concrete poetry poetry in which the shape made by the words on the page fits their meaning.

conjunctions link words, used to join parts of a sentence together (e.g. The goods train *and* the express were a mile apart *but* were coming closer by the second.).

dialect a style of English used in one area, or in other English-speaking countries. Dialects differ from **standard English** in **grammar** (e.g. word order) and **vocabulary** (actual words used; e.g. *grockle*, a West Country word for a tourist).

dialogue conversation in a novel, story or play.

direct speech actual words spoken, given in **speech marks**.

drafting producing an improved version of a piece of writing.

emotive language language used to stir up the reader's emotions (e.g. The mechanical diggers *gouged a deep wound* in the green hillside.).

epic a long poem describing the deeds of a legendary hero. See also **legends**.

fact a piece of information which can be proven and is generally agreed to be true.

feature a one-off magazine article, as opposed to a regular article such as the horoscope.

fiction made-up stories.

form the category into which a piece of writing falls (e.g. a leaflet, a play, a novel).

formality the level of seriousness in the style of language, usually depending on the situation. For example, you would use formal language in an interview.

grammar the rules by which we order and combine different types of words in sentences.

histories plays, especially by Shakespeare, based on historical fact (e.g. *Julius Caesar* and *Henry V*).

hot-seating an exercise in which one person answers questions as if they were a particular character in a novel or play.

image a word picture used to make an idea come alive (e.g. a **metaphor**, **simile**, or **personification**).

imagery the kind of word picture used to make an idea come alive.

legends old stories, usually involving good and evil, gods, heroes and heroines, which were originally based on real events.

media the means of mass communication: especially newspapers, television, radio and the Internet.

metaphor a description of a thing as if it were something different but also in some way similar (e.g. He *hammered* the ball into the open goal.).

metre in poetry, a set pattern of **rhythm** and number of **syllables** in a line.

monologue a long speech by one character.

myth an old story, usually involving gods and humankind, which was passed down from one generation to the next and developed on the way. Myths are not historically true, but they can contain hidden meaning.

narrative story-telling. See also **viewpoint**.

narrator a person telling a story.

noun a word for a thing. This could be a thing you could touch, such as a dog, a bike or a house; or something abstract, such as freedom, love, hate or happiness. Names of people and places are called *proper nouns*.

onomatopoeia the use of a word whose sound echoes its meaning (e.g. *ping-pong*; *miaow*; *thud*).

open question a question which invites more than a yes/no answer (e.g. How do you feel?) See also **closed question**.

opinion a viewpoint; for how this differs from a fact, see page 85.

oxymoron a kind of **image** which combines opposites (e.g. a *tiny giant* of a man.).

parts of speech the different types of words used in sentences: nouns, verbs, adjectives, adverbs, pronouns, prepositions and conjunctions (see separate entries).

personification a description of something as if it were a person (e.g. *Time marches* on.).

plot the storyline of a novel, story or play.

prepositions short words which come before other **parts of speech** to tell us where, when or how something happens: e.g. *in* the rain; *by* train; *for* years; *near* a road; *before* the match.

pronouns words which take the place of **nouns** (e.g. he, she, it).

proofreading the final stage of writing in which you check for mistakes in spelling, punctuation and **grammar**.

prose written language with no fixed **rhythm**, **metre** or **rhyme**.

pun a play on similar-sounding words whose meanings are appropriate in different ways (e.g. I've just had to change my *tyre*, and now I'm *tired* out!).

register the style of speech appropriate to a particular situation. This depends on *who* we are speaking to, *what* we are speaking about, and *why* we are speaking.

reported speech the report of what someone said, rather than their exact words (e.g. *She asked* if I wanted an ice cream.). Also called indirect speech.

rhyme when two words begin with different sounds and end in the same sound: e.g. fish, dish.

rhythm in poetry, the pattern of speed variations that the **syllables** in a line force you to make as you say the line.

scanning the kind of fast reading in which you look for something in particular (e.g. looking for pizza on a restaurant menu).

scene a division of a play smaller than an Act. In a scene, all the action is in one place.

selection (form of bias) in writing, including only those **facts** that fit your **opinion**.

setting the place in which the action of a story occurs, which usually affects the atmosphere (e.g. the wild moor where the Witches meet in Shakespeare's *Macbeth*).

simile an image comparing things which are different in most ways but similar in one way, usually with 'like' or 'as' (e.g. Mrs Jones burst into the room *like* a volcano on legs.).

skimming the kind of fast reading in which you try to get a general idea of what a passage is about.

soliloquy a speech made by one actor alone on stage, especially in Shakespeare.

speech marks quotation marks; punctuation marks used before and after the actual words someone says (e.g. '*You're fired!*' she exploded.).

stage direction a note from a playwright in a play saying what the actors should do, or how a line should be spoken.

standard English the most widely understood style of English, spoken by all those who want to be understood by strangers or the general public, such as newsreaders or politicians. It can be spoken in any **accent**, but cannot include **dialect**.

structure how a **plot** is organised.

syllable the smallest pronounceable part of word (e.g. *elephant* has three syllables).

synonym a word meaning the same as another word (e.g. *huge* for *enormous*).

target audience the particular kind of people at whom a magazine, leaflet or advertisement is aimed.

tenses the forms of a verb which show *when* something is happening (e.g. I go, I went, I will go).

theme an idea explored by an author (e.g. time, or revenge).

tragedies plays focusing on a tragic hero or heroine (e.g. *Macbeth*; *Romeo and Juliet*).

verbs doing words (e.g. swim, laugh, run, play, remember).

viewpoint how a story is told (e.g. through action, or in discussion between minor characters). A novel could be in the first person ('I climbed over the fence ...') or third person ('She climbed over the fence ...').

vocabulary the range of words used in speech or writing.

Index

BUZAN TRAINING COURSES